BE HAPPILY MARRIED

Even If Your Partner
Won't Do a Thing

ABBY MEDCALF, PH.D.

Copyright © 2019 Abby Medcalf Thriving, LLC

All rights reserved. No part of this publication may be reproduced, distributed, or transmitted in any form or by any means, including photocopying, recording, or other electronic or mechanical methods, without the prior written permission of the publisher, except in the case of brief quotations embodied in reviews and certain other noncommercial uses permitted by copyright law.

www.abbymedcalf.com

For orders or inquiries, please use the form on the website.

This book will give you everything you need to create a happy, connected and fulfilled relationship, even if your partner won't do a thing. But, for those of you looking for even more, you can download my free *Be Happily Married Tool Kit* at *www.abbymedcalf.com/bonustoolkit*.

"Abby was the 7th couples' therapist we tried. I wish she had been our first. We wouldn't have wasted all that money and time on the other six. We read her book, followed the clear tips she outlines and our relationship was completely transformed." – **Eric G.**

"Thank you for this book Abby. We're so grateful to you. It's not just our marriage you saved. But our family. When I look into my children's eyes, I thank you." – **Elisa M.**

"I was never able to stick with things before. Then I read Abby's book. Now I've got new ways of acting and being in my relationship and I've changed my marriage for good." – **Andrea J.**

"Finally! A book that makes sense! You really can make changes without rehashing your whole relationship or working on it for hours a week! Why doesn't everyone do it this way?" – **Janice O.**

"This book is like marriage cliff notes!" – **Tess B.**

"I didn't believe that I really could change my relationship because my husband refused to do anything. After reading Abby's book and using her simple tips, my relationship feels more connected and happy. I'm a believer!" – **Saanvi G.**

"I've read every book out there but this is the one that worked. I'd lost hope and didn't think I'd ever really have a happy marriage. My husband and I were actually laughing together the other day – that hasn't happened in years...I wish I'd read this book years ago." – **Teresa T**

"Read the book, follow the clear steps, and there's no way you won't see positive changes within a few short weeks!" – **Jonathan B**

DEDICATION

This book is dedicated to all the clients I've served. I never could've written this book without you. Your honesty, openness, courage and willingness to keep trying helped me figure out what truly works to create happy, connected and fulfilled relationships, even if your partner won't do a thing.

TABLE OF CONTENTS

Acknowledgments 11
Introduction 13
Chapter One: This is the Last Relationship
Book You'll Ever Have to Read 15
Chapter Two: Just How Committed Are You? 27
Chapter Three: Self-Awareness 37
Chapter Four - Key #2: The Importance
of Answering Bids 51
Chapter Five - Key #3: Set an Intention of Kindness 61
Chapter Six - Key #4: Be Vulnerable
(It's not as scary as you think) 71
Chapter Seven - Key #5: Your Lizard Brain and
Why You Need to Say "Yes" First 79
Chapter Eight - Key #6: Ask Questions and
Don't SAC Your Relationship 95
Chapter Nine - Key #7: Bring Your Sexy Back 107
Chapter Ten - Key #8: Be Positive 119
Chapter Eleven - Key #9: Keeping Score in
Your Relationship Makes You Lose 131
Chapter Twelve - KEY 10: Forgiveness 141
Conclusion 157
Author Biography 159

ACKNOWLEDGMENTS

I'm so grateful for all the support I've received personally and professionally so I could write this book. On a personal note, I'd like to thank my incredible man, Gary. Your unwavering support and faith in me means so much. I simply couldn't ask for a better partner to go through life with. I'd also like to thank my awesome children, Max and Macartney, for being so understanding and loving as I took time away from you to work on this book. Finally, a shout out to my league of besties who support me in every imaginable way: Rhonda Davis, Stephanie Baer-Spoden, Suzette DeWinter, and Rochelle Lenahan.

Professionally, I'd like to acknowledge my fabulous coach, Jadah Sellner; my colleague in crime, Tess Brigham; my spot-on publisher, Azul Terronez; my inspiring consulting group, Scott, Tim, Andy, Dave and Stephanie; and my awesome Online Empire Manager, Brigid Ward.

INTRODUCTION

Welcome to my world—I'm so happy you're here!

The book you're reading is the culmination of over 25 years of working with individuals and couples who wanted to create lasting changes in their relationships.

My goal is, above all, to provide practical, usable tools that WORK—not unproven ideas or pie-in-the-sky theories that sound good but do little to help you in your day-to-day life. I use my hands-on experience and my background in both psychology and business (and my humor) to create tips and tools that work to transform any relationship into a connected communication machine, even if your partner won't do a thing.

Each of the chapters in this book is another key to your success. I know you're probably in a rush to get started, but I'm going to ask you to make sure you read each chapter thoroughly and take the time to figure out how you're going to incorporate each chapter's Action Tips into your daily life.

As you read, you'll see that this book is written from the point of view of married, heterosexual couples, since that's about 70 percent of my practice. *However*, this information applies liberally to anyone attempting a long-term partnership, including those who aren't married, the polyamorous and gay or lesbian couples. So, if you're trying to be in a romantic relationship, no matter who you are, this book can help.

The 10 Keys to Being Happily Married

At the end of the day, there's really nothing more important than your relationship with your significant other. Think about it: you can have a great day at work, but if your home is filled with tension and hostility, your life will suck. However, even if you have a crappy day at work or out in the world, if you come home and it feels peaceful and loving, your life will feel satisfying and whole. Knowing this, how can you NOT make your relationship your priority?

Ready to create an amazing relationship? It's time to dive in!

Looking forward to hearing all about your success,

Abby

CHAPTER ONE

THIS IS THE LAST RELATIONSHIP BOOK YOU'LL EVER HAVE TO READ

If you're reading this, it's likely not the first thing you've tried to improve your relationship. Maybe you've been to couples' counseling, attended a workshop, read blog posts, taken notes from other books and looked at every video with the hashtag #HappyMarriage you could find.

You've done these things, you made some changes, but soon found yourself backsliding into old behavior and repeating negative patterns. You're thinking things like

- "I can't make my relationship better because my partner refuses to make any changes."
- "Why can't we ever make changes that stick?!"
- "This is going to take too long. We've been this way for years, and I don't have the energy to work on this for the next decade!"
- "I already have so much on my plate; I can't imagine fitting in one more thing!"

All of this thinking is wrong. (Yeah, I said it.) The reason you've been struggling is due to three crucial factors that I'm going to explain to you right now. Once you understand these components, **you'll see why this book is completely different than any other relationship book and why it can be the last relationship book you'll ever have to read!** You're going to learn how to *easily* create the happy and connected relationship you've been craving (and it won't take a ton of your time).

Reason #1
You Haven't Been Successful Before:

Your first problem is that you've been basing your life on the idea that there are 24 hours in a day. You look at each day, see all the things you need to get done, and divide all this by the hours you've got. Work, taking care of kids, grocery shopping, volunteering for your kid's bake sale at school, commuting, going to the gym and cleaning up your house (and yourself) all get fit into a schedule for the day. You likely end each day feeling exhausted, overwhelmed, and with half the things on your to-do list left *undone*. (No, I don't have hidden cameras in your house.)

With thinking like this, *it's no wonder* you have no energy for sex, self-care or all the amazing ideas outlined in great books like this! The secret to ending this hopeless cycle is to *stop thinking of your day based on 24 hours.*

Instead, I want you to think of your day as being comprised of Apps. I'm about to rock your world with a whole new way of looking at it, so give me a minute to explain.

I want you to think of your brain as being like your smartphone. Right now, you've got a bunch of Apps on your phone. Some of these Apps take up a lot of space and drain the battery on your phone quickly. Others are smaller, but still do their share of wearing down that energy source.

The Apps on your phone are things like your calendar, solitaire and iTunes. The Apps in your brain are equivalent to ALL the things you've got going on in your day-to-day life: work, commuting, getting kids shuttled around, grocery shopping, cleaning, eating, basic self-care (if you've even got that on your list), answering your emails and returning phone calls (do people even do that anymore?).

Now, there are also a *bunch* of Apps running in the background of your brain. You know how you've got to "quit" the Apps on your phone or they'll drain your battery? Well, the same is true for all these "hidden" Apps in your life that are secretly draining your energy: your aging mom in Florida, that root canal you've been putting off, the gray hair you found this morning (and it wasn't even on your head!), whether Johnny will get picked for the baseball team, the school auction you volunteered for, that 10 pounds you want to lose, getting summer camps and vacations scheduled, the fact that you spent too much money yesterday, that big project at work, that bitch Barbara at work, the fight you had last week with your sister… need I go on?!?!

Just like the Apps on your phone, all these Apps in your life are draining you.

Now, the battery on your smartphone is made up of electronic stuff. The battery that is YOU is made up of willpower. That's right. All these Apps in your life run on your willpower.

Let me tell you a few things about willpower. Willpower is the control you exert to do anything or resist any impulses. A happy, balanced, meaningful life is all about resisting urges and impulses. Want to be productive? You've got to resist the urge to scroll through Facebook (again) or check that alert on your phone while you're busy with something else. Want to lose weight? You've got to resist the cravings for unhealthy foods all day or resist the urge to keep eating the rest of that donut after you've had one bite. Want to get to the gym? You've got to resist the yearning to go back to sleep in the morning when your alarm goes off at an ungodly hour or resist the inclination to sit on your couch binge-watching *This is Us*.

Your willpower is at the center of all this. The problem is that *your willpower is an exhaustible resource*. This means that you wake up each morning with a certain amount of willpower and, as your day goes on, you start draining that willpower battery with all the Apps you've got running (*even those Apps you don't realize you're thinking about*).

> You exhaust your willpower with every single decision and frustration you have all day. The more you've got to think, the more it drains. The more annoyed, worried or anxious you are, the more your willpower battery is drained.

Habits are a big part of willpower. Habits are things you *don't* have to think much about because, by definition, these are things you do automatically. While healthy habits *add* to your willpower allowance for the day, unhealthy habits *take away* from your daily willpower allotment.

Let's take working out. This is a healthy habit that will definitely add to your willpower. Monday through Friday, I wake up very early and go to the gym. I've been doing it for a few years, so now it's a habit. When the alarm goes off in the morning, *I don't decide to get up and work out*. **It's already decided**—I don't think, I just do.

Now, I am NOT someone who likes working out. As a matter of fact, I tried to get my butt to exercise for years, with no consistent success. That alarm would go off way too early and my first thoughts were: "NOOOOOO! Why did I think I wanted to get up this early? I need to sleep." At which point, I'd promptly turn off my alarm or hit the snooze button 27 times.

How did I finally make this one stick? I realized I was draining my willpower on too many fronts and had too many Apps open. To be successful, I needed to close some Apps and not drain my willpower with so many new habits at the same time.

For example, I realized I was always trying to eat perfectly whenever I started a workout plan. I would add all these new, stressful things to my life at once: going to the gym (How do I work these machines? What *exactly* should I even do when I get there? Do I look stupid? I hate all these mirrors highlighting my ass!). Then I added my new diet (What should I eat and when? I needed to grocery shop, figure out how to cook these new foods, look at recipes and make things that my family would still like). On top of that, since I was waking up earlier to work out, I needed to get to bed earlier the night before (or at least try), so I felt more pressure to get things done quicker each evening (kids to bed, clean the dishes, answer emails). It was all too much!!

So, I decided to just focus on one new thing at a time (working out) and to get help to make me accountable so it would be easier to stick to my new habit. I stopped trying to eat perfectly and added a personal trainer. The trainer decided when I would work out, how often and what we were doing. I only needed to show up (very little willpower used there). I kept the trainer for three months (more about why I did it for three months in a minute). It was expensive, but I knew it wasn't forever. It was a short-term investment in myself.

I was also very clear with the trainer that we were *not* going to talk about my food, weigh me or anything else. The goal was to have workouts that I could do on my own *easily* at the end of the three months. No new-fangled apparatus every workout, no changes every single session. Just clear, simple things that I could do later on my own. Adding help, shrinking the change to as few variables as possible and taking away other new things were the keys to my success.

> The big secret that's been undermining *your success* is this: when you're learning a new habit, even a healthy one like working out, meditating, eating well or practicing what you learned in a self-help book, *it drains your willpower!* It's because you have to think so much and constantly redirect yourself.

If you're starting to eat a healthy breakfast, that's great. However, *it's going to sap your willpower initially*. Until it becomes a habit, it drains your willpower instead of adding to it! Cooking new food, deciding what to eat, shopping for the groceries when you haven't before and redirecting yourself from your impulse to eat a big bagel all put a strain on your willpower.

You know that, eventually, eating a healthy breakfast is going to really improve your life: you'll have more energy, your day will start off on a good food-note, which means you'll likely eat better for the rest of the day, and you'll lose weight (according to a huge amount of research).

In the end, if you make eating a healthy breakfast a habit, it will absolutely improve your life and *increase* your willpower! It's a great thing to do. However, *until eating a healthy breakfast becomes a habit, it will drain your willpower*.

It's the same with what you're going through right now. Your relationship is a huge App that's draining you on so many levels. Getting it to a happy, connected and satisfying place will TOTALLY improve your life, happiness and energy level. However, doing the work to get there is going to initially put more strain on your life.

The mistake most people make when they look to improve their relationship is they add stuff that they need to do themselves, so they add stress: they add reading a book, date nights, couples' counseling, etc. But where does this go in your already *very* full life? There's no room to add if you're the one doing the legwork!

When individuals or couples come to my office, the first thing I ask them is, "What are you going to take *off* your plate, so you can work on your relationship?" They mistakenly think that making the commitment to the time it takes to come to therapy is their only priority.

> *They account for the time, but not for the Apps.*

It doesn't need to be hard to change your relationship, but it *does* take concerted, consistent effort. Where is that bandwidth going to come from? You need room in your head to think about and mentally incorporate these new concepts, not just the time to practice them.

Think about how many times you've told yourself you'll finish some project, go to the gym or meet up with friends on some weeknight. You work all day at whatever you do: You commute, make decisions, prepare, worry and run around. You get home, eat dinner and have the whole night in front of you. By 7:00pm, however, most folks are mentally exhausted. Yes, you still have "time," or hours, until you go to bed, but all you want to do is binge-watch something on Netflix and eat the things you didn't allow yourself all day. (Again, no, I don't have hidden cameras in your home.)

> *It's not about the time in your day, it's about the mind in your day!*

It's about your emotional resources; your mental capacity to handle "one more thing." Your willpower has just drained out and there's no gas left in the tank for sex, dinner with friends or going to the gym.

Having an awesome relationship is all about incorporating new skills that become habits. Effective communication is a skill, listening is a skill, patience is a skill, and self-confidence is a skill. When you practice these skills over time, they become healthy habits and ways of being in your relationship. But creating habits takes time.

How much time? How long does it actually take to form a new habit (in this case, having the habits you need to create an amazing relationship)? The answer is from a woman named Phillippa Lally. She's a health psychology researcher at the University College London and is the bomb-diggity when it comes to research on habits. Her extensive studies show that *it takes an average of 66 days to break/create a habit*.[1] Since this is the *average*, I tell folks to give themselves three months.

Right now, I need you to ask yourself, "What am I going to take *off* my plate for the next three months so I have the bandwidth to work on my relationship?" This could mean hiring a cleaning person (or using one more often or asking

---

1 *https://onlinelibrary.wiley.com/doi/abs/10.1002/ejsp.674*

them to also do the laundry), asking someone to carpool your kids to school, changing your work schedule to leave at 3:00pm, getting a gardener, having groceries delivered, telling the school you need to bow out of the yearly bake sale, hiring a dog walker (or making your kids do it) or saying "no" to anything that gets asked of you over the next three months.

You've really got to do this if you want to be successful. You can't just add "working on my relationship" to your already-overflowing to-do list and expect it to work. *It's got to be a priority for the next three months* and you need to make a commitment, which means getting other things off your plate.

Right now, I want you to identify the three things you'll take *off* your plate for the next three months:

1. _____

2. _____

3. _____

Reason #2
You Haven't Been Successful Before:

The next reason why this can be the last book you'll ever read about how to have a happy relationship is that I'm not only giving you a fish (this book), I'm going to *teach you how to fish*. Every chapter will have Action Items at the end. These are specific and easy-to-apply techniques to incorporate each of the ten keys into your daily life. There's no journaling for five hours, long date nights where all you're thinking about is the pressure to have sex later, or costly things to incorporate.

The Action Items are all the best tools that I've been using with my clients (and myself) for years. These are the ones that work because they're easy to understand, don't take a lot of time and are super effective with lots of bang for your buck (when you end up having more sex because of these tools, you'll see how there's a great pun in there).

For those of you overachievers out there (or those who get bored easily), I'm also including bonus tips that you can access on my website at *www.abbymedcalf.com/bonustoolkit*

Reason #3
You Haven't Been Successful Before:

The last reason this can be the last book on relationships you read is because, if you bought this, your focus is in the right place: YOU.

I've been working with couples for decades now, and I noticed something amazing about seven years ago. Although I've had incredible success with couples when they come in together, I've had the same level of success, *if not higher*, with individuals who come in alone because their partner has refused to come or do any work! What?!?!?

Yes! You can completely change your relationship, even if your partner won't lift a finger, read a book, go to counseling or admit they have a problem. Let me tell you why you can transform your relationship into a connectivity, passion-generating machine *even if your partner won't do a single thing*.

Have you ever walked down the street and saw someone coming at you that caught your attention in a bad way? The person didn't necessarily say or do anything, but you noticed yourself focusing on them and could just feel some negative vibe coming off of them? Maybe you ended up crossing the street or keeping your eye on them because you could "just tell" something was off or something bad could happen?

This is because you're picking up on that person's intentions. This is just like when your partner comes home and you can tell they're in a bad mood before they say anything. Your unconscious mind is powerful and it's picking up what the other person is laying down!

Research shows that your conscious brain processes information at a rate of approximately 50 bits per second (don't ask me what a "bit" is). Meanwhile, your *unconscious* mind processes information at a rate of 11 million bits per second. That's not a typo. That's 50 versus 11 million!![2] Your unconscious mind is on the job and it's affecting what your conscious mind is processing all the time.

When you get into a head space that you're going to change your relationship, even if your partner won't do a thing, you start sending out very different signals, both consciously and unconsciously. Your partner picks up on these signals (both consciously and unconsciously themselves) and the results are astounding! Your partner will start reacting differently even when they don't realize what's changed. I've seen it again and again.

This is going to be so empowering for you. Instead of feeling resentful and irritated with your partner, you'll start to feel confident, self-assured, patient and compassionate. You'll focus each day on yourself and what *you're* doing, instead of what *they're* doing. The focus on what your partner is doing is what leaves you feeling frustrated, hopeless and resentful. *You can't build a loving relationship on any of these emotions.* **You are where your attention is!**

---

[2] https://www.amazon.com/Sweet-Spot-Accomplish-More-Doing/dp/0553392069

Your new intention, which I'll talk about a lot more in Chapter Five, will set the tone for your relationship and everything will change from there.

> You have the complete power to
> change what you're doing and thinking,
> so you have the complete power to
> change your life and your relationship.

Imagine communicating, laughing, feeling appreciated and having a sense of kindness and compassion in your relationship. All these things are possible, *and you can do it in the next three months if you make it your priority.*

CHAPTER TWO

JUST HOW COMMITTED ARE YOU?

Marriage. Long-term relationship. Life partner. For some, these words bring feelings of warmth and longing and, for others, feelings of terror and thoughts of running far away. What's up with marriage? Why are we still doing it when there's a divorce every 36 seconds, adding up to a little over 800,000 divorces a year?![3]

The divorce "rate" (and this is a hotly contested statistic) is most commonly cited as hovering somewhere around 50% (and the divorce rate for second and third marriages is even higher).[4] As if that's not bad enough, just quoting divorce rates is misleading because it doesn't even take into account *the millions of couples who stay together but are miserable.* In his book *The Science of Happily Ever After*, psychologist Ty Tashiro[5] notes that only three in ten married couples stay in "healthy, happy marriages." It seems that happy long-term marriages are becoming the stuff of folklore and myth, like

---

3   *http://www.cdc.gov/nchs/nvss/marriage_divorce_tables.htm* and *http://www.pewsocialtrends.org/2013/02/13/love-and-marriage/*
4   http://www.apa.org/topics/divorce/
5   *https://www.amazon.com/Science-Happily-Ever-After-Enduring/dp/037389290X*

spotting Bigfoot: "I've definitely seen one; I don't have any proof exactly, but I've seen it."

If being happily married was a business, it would have somewhere around a 70 percent failure rate. Knowing this, doesn't it seem crazy that anyone would ever apply for a job there? Yet, each June, the most popular wedding month of the year, some 13,000 couples will say "I do" in the United States.[6] Hopeful men and women will stand in churches, synagogues, fields, court houses, backyards and parks committing to a lifelong relationship.

People still get married because, despite all the doom and gloom written about marriage and long-term relationships, research has shown over and over that marriage still brings many benefits. For example, married people[7]

- Enjoy better health (they're less likely to have strokes or heart disease and they heal more quickly),
- Have more sound mental health (they have less depression and better responses to stress),
- Have more money and assets (divorced women have the highest poverty rates among women in the US),[8] and (shock!),
- Enjoy better sex lives than folks who remain single.

And here's something else really cool. *The longer couples stay together, the more "in love" they eventually become!* Eminent marriage researcher Dr. John Gottman says, "The surprising thing is that the longer people are together, the more the sense of kindness returns. Our research is starting to reveal

---

6   http://www.cdc.gov/nchs/fastats/marriage-divorce.htm
7   *http://www.nytimes.com/1995/04/10/us/studies-find-big-benefits-in-marriage.html*
8   https://www.ssa.gov/policy/docs/ssb/v72n1/v72n1p11.html

that in later life, your relationship becomes very much like it was during courtship."[9]

The big question you're likely asking right now is, "That's great, but how do I get from where I am, to way over there?" How do you get to that warm fuzzy "in love" place again (or for the first time)? And how do you do it if your partner refuses to get off the couch or read this book?

With over 60 years of hard research and thousands of studies, there's actually some good news. There are some consistent themes identified in the research, some "keys" to staying happily married for the long term. If you do these things, you'll see the nature of your relationship change. Your partner will start reacting differently to you, *because you're acting differently*!

Think about if you're in a bad mood or snap at your partner. Doesn't this change your partner's behavior? Don't they maybe snap back at you, ignore you or act disgusted or angry? You change your partner's behavior all the time without even thinking about it! It happens the other way, too. Maybe you're in a great mood, but then your partner comes home and is surly or makes a nasty remark. Doesn't this change your thinking and actions? Of course it does! In this book, you're going to learn to harness this energy and use it to *improve* your relationship instead of hurting it.

From the research and my own extensive, hands-on experience, I've identified ten keys to being happily married. In each of the ten chapters, you'll learn the research, get a Real-Life Example of how it works, and then be taught specific, simple Action Tips for operationalizing the keys into your life. Ideas are great, but if you can't figure out how to use or apply them, they don't do much good. I'm all about

---

[9] http://www.theatlantic.com/health/archive/2014/06/happily-ever-after/372573/

having actionable tools you can use *today* to improve your relationship and start seeing results. The kicker: none of the tools requires hours of work. All of them can be incorporated in just a few minutes a day (really!).

> If you haven't read the chapter before this, you need to go back and read it now. It explains why you've failed before to improve your relationship, and why this time can absolutely be different!

I want to say one last word about commitment before we jump in. There's a quote on the wall in my office that says, "The difference between involvement and commitment is like a breakfast of ham and eggs: the chicken is involved but the pig is committed."

I've got it there because a lot of people over the years have come into my office fed up with their relationship and ready to leave. They say things like: "I'm going to see how the therapy goes and then decide whether I'm going to stay in the relationship." I tell them right then that they might as well not come to therapy because it's not going to work if that's their thinking.

The commitment needs to come first. Commit to stay together and do the work. When you have one foot in and one foot out, you're not going to have a successful, long-term outcome.

If you were at a job with one foot in and one foot out, wouldn't people pick up on your energy? Wouldn't you be acting a certain way and viewing things differently than if you were completely committed? Would you expect raises or promotions with this kind of attitude and focus? Do you see the parallel? It really is the same with your partner.

In his research, Dr. Karl Pillemer of Cornell University found that in successful marriages, "People really had the mindset they wanted to stay married. They regarded their partnership as less like buying a new car and more like learning to drive. Marriage is like a discipline. A discipline is not reaching one happy endpoint."[10]

> Commitment is like training for a race. Training doesn't guarantee you'll win, but you still get a whole bunch of advantages and value out of it, even if you don't.

"When people say, 'I'm committed to my relationship,' they can mean [different] things," says Benjamin Karney, a professor of psychology and co-director of the Relationship Institute at UCLA.[11] In studies at the Relationship Institute, they've found that those couples with a deeper level of commitment and a willingness to make sacrifices for the sake of the marriage have lower divorce rates and report fewer problems in their marriages. This mindset works even if you're the only one who seems committed and the only one doing any of the work.

Another researcher at the Relationship Institute says it well: "When we're under a great deal of stress or when there is a high-stakes decision on which you disagree, those are defining moments in a relationship. What our data indicate is

---

10   https://www.amazon.com/30-Lessons-Loving-Americans-Relationships/dp/1594631549
11   *http://marriage.psych.ucla.edu/research.html).*

that committing to the relationship rather than committing to your own agenda and your own immediate needs is a far better strategy."[12] I'm going to teach you how to do just that in this book.

If you want a happy and satisfying long-term relationship, you need to start with your commitment.

Now, you might be saying, "But my partner isn't willing to make any sacrifices. They won't do the work!"

I say to that, "It begins with you." Someone has to take these concrete steps first and stick with them!

You might be saying, "But I've tried so many times, and although we initially make some headway, we eventually fall back into old patterns and nothing ever sticks!" First, I hear your pain. Second, I'm going to ask you to really think about these changes you've made in the past.

Here's what usually happens. You make some changes, maybe you're nicer to your partner, maybe you start paying attention or maybe you start doing more things for them. Whatever it is, your partner sees the changes, *but doesn't trust them*. They're thinking (either consciously or unconsciously) something like, "Oh, *now* s/he's being nice to me. Let's see how long *that* lasts." So, your partner doesn't seem like they appreciate the changes or doesn't make any changes themselves because they don't trust what's happening. They think it's going to go away soon, so why bother getting their hopes up or putting in any effort? You see or feel this response and say things like, "See, nothing works!" Then, you stop with your new behaviors and the two of you are back to your old, negative cycle.

---

12 *http://newsroom.ucla.edu/releases/here-is-what-real-commitment-to-228064*

This time is different. This time, you're going to stick to your changes for three months. *No matter what your partner does or doesn't do, you're going to stick to your plan because you're committed.* For these three months, there's no back and forth, no wavering, just full-on commitment.

Let me ask you something, have you ever tried to lose a little weight? You diet, grocery shop, exercise and do everything right but the needle on the scale doesn't move at all? Sometimes you even *gain* weight initially!?!? This is just like that. You know that if you had stuck to your plan for a longer period of time, eventually the weight *would* have come off, barring any underlying serious medical problems. The issue is that you wanted to see immediate results and you didn't commit to the long-term goal for long enough. We all like to see immediate results for our labor and can give up when we don't see progress right away.

It's the same here. You've just got to stick with your behavior and thought changes, even if you don't see any immediate results, because, eventually, things will change. They might be small, incremental changes, but they'll eventually add up.

If you continue to eat well and exercise, eventually, the needle on the scale will start to move in the right direction. If you continue to change your behaviors with your partner, eventually the needle on *that* scale will move in the right direction, too.

Success is usually about choosing between what you want right now and what you want most.

The 10 Keys to Being Happily Married

You've got to stay motivated to stick to your goal. How do you do this? *When you feel like you want to quit, you've got to remember why you started.* Pain motivates us more than pleasure, so I want you to take a minute right now and list three pain points you have in your relationship. These are the three things that, when they're resolved, you'll feel SOOOO happy and great in your life and relationship. These are the things that you hate *the most* about your relationship. These are the things you complain about, that keep you up at night and that motivated you to buy this book.

Write your three pain points here:

1. *Walking on eggshells*
2. *Sex*
3. *Stuck in UK*

Now, I want you to close your eyes and think about that first pain point. That first issue that you've just got to fix so you can feel happier in your relationship. Think of having that issue totally resolved. How would you be feeling? I want you to write down three sentences about how you'll feel when this is no longer an issue in your relationship. Imagine the freedom, happiness, ease, relief, laughter, fulfillment, confidence, joy or whatever you'd be feeling and write three sentences about that here:

How I'll feel when my first pain point is OVER:

1. *Relaxed / relieved*
2. *Closer to wife*
3. *Happier to be at home*

Now, I'd like you to do that same exercise with your second and third pain points. Take the time to do this right now. It'll take less than 10 minutes and is TOTALLY worth it!

How I'll feel when my second pain point is OVER:
1. _Close to wife_
2. _Fulfilled (not missing big part of life)_
3. _Confident / more self worth_

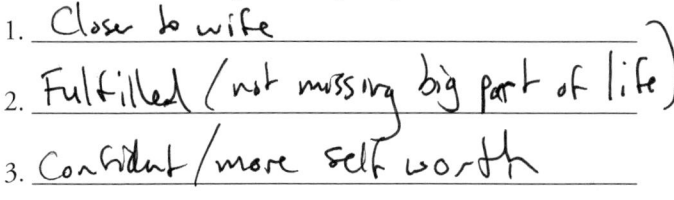

How I'll feel when my third pain point is OVER:
1. _Free (not trapped)_
2. _Fulfilled (reach career/life goals)_
3. _Excited (new adventures)_

The next time you're feeling like quitting or giving up, I want you to come back to these three pain points and how you'll feel when they're no longer an issue. This is your key to motivating yourself to stick with your commitment over the next three months.

I've been clean from a bad drug addiction for many years now. There's a saying we have in Narcotics Anonymous: "Half measures availed us nothing." That fits perfectly here. It's time to go all in. Balls to the wall (boobs to the wall if you're a woman reading this?). It's time to change your relationship, even if your partner won't do a thing.

CHAPTER THREE

SELF-AWARENESS

You have to have a healthy relationship with yourself before you can have a healthy relationship with anyone else. I don't mean that you have to love your thighs in order to really love your partner (since no woman would ever get married again if this was a requirement).

What I *do* mean is that you have to be able to look at yourself objectively and know your strengths and limitations. You have to know when you're reacting because you're hearing your mother's voice inside your head instead of your partner's voice in real life. You have to be able to pull back when the real reason you're upset with your partner is because you're tired and hungry and *not* because your partner made the HUGE, clearly divorce-worthy mistake of leaving the cap off the toothpaste (I'm being sarcastic— if you didn't get that, you need to read faster).

Self-awareness is the key to realizing that *you* are responsible for your own happiness.[13] Your partner is not (I hated learning this, too, but it doesn't make it any less true). The more you feel the need to focus on your partner, the more you need to focus on yourself and your *own* actions and thoughts. You do this by learning to train your attention to be in the moment, and not on what's happened in the past

13   http://www.wilsonlab.com/publications/2016_JHSE_McGill_et_al.pdf

or what you think might happen in the future. The obstacle to being and thinking in the "here and now" is distraction.[14]

Distraction is the termites eating at the foundation of your relationship.

For example, you might be talking to your partner about his difficult day at work, but your mind is distracted as you think of what you need to make for dinner and whether it's your turn to carpool tomorrow. Or maybe you're walking the dog, but you're not thinking about how nice a morning it is or how great the breeze feels on your face. Instead, you're thinking about the project you need to finish for work and whether or not that was *your* hair in the sink this morning.

All of this mind-wandering leads to misunderstandings, frustration, anger, unhappiness and resentment. The problem is that your mind wanders *a lot*. In fact, research shows it wanders about 47 percent of the time! Depending on what you're doing, your mind wanders from a high of about 65 percent (doing things like taking a shower or brushing your teeth) down to a low of about 10 percent when you're having sex (this scared me a little to think that even 10 percent of the time my man is thinking about mowing the grass when I'm naked with him, but I try not to let my mind wander there too often). There's also stuff in between (your mind wanders about 50 percent of the time at work and about 40 percent of the time when you're exercising).[15]

---

14   *http://www.ncbi.nlm.nih.gov/pubmed/17935531*
15   https://greatergood.berkeley.edu/article/item/does_mind_wandering_make_you_unhappy

The bottom line: mind-wandering affects *everything* you do. So, how does all this wandering relate to your happiness? Research by Matt Killingsworth[16] found that *you're significantly less happy when your mind wanders*. How often your mind wanders and what you think about when it does is totally predictive of how happy you feel (way more than how much money you make or the size of your house or ass, for example).

When your mind is wandering, you're likely thinking of unpleasant things, playing something negative over and over in your head or thinking about regrets, worries or anxieties.

Maybe you're worried your partner is cheating and you're playing the movie of them laughing at dinner with someone else, or maybe you're thinking of all the things you "should" have said when you were defending yourself in last night's argument. Maybe you're just thinking about what a jerk your partner is and how they don't understand or appreciate you.

For the record, even mind-wandering about neutral or happy things is shown to lower baseline happiness levels. In other words, no matter what you're mind-wandering about, it's a downer to some degree.

What does all this have to do with being happier in your relationship? All that mind-wandering is causing fights, misunderstandings and miscommunications. This real-life example will bring home what I'm saying.

---

16   https://news.harvard.edu/gazette/story/2010/11/wandering-mind-not-a-happy-mind/

REAL-LIFE EXAMPLE

Let me give you an excellent example told to me by a woman I worked with named Shelly (we're changing real names throughout this book to protect the innocent).

Once upon a time, Shelly and her husband, Jake, needed to get a tree taken down in front of their home. They both agreed that it would be a good idea for Shelly to call because the "tree guy" liked her better and would be more likely to come do the job quicker.

About two weeks after this joint decision, Shelly was in the shower and Jake walked into the bathroom and asked (innocently enough) if she'd called the tree guy. Now, before I tell you what she answered, I want you to know that Shelly was going to be very busy that day because she was leaving on a business trip and had a ton to do before she left. Shelly was standing there, washing her hair, but she wasn't really in the shower. She wasn't thinking about how good it felt to be massaging in the shampoo or leaning in to the nice, warm water. No, she was thinking about the ten billion things (yes, I said billion) she needed to do before she left. Shelly was distracted and not in the "here and now."

Poor, unknowing Jake chose this moment to walk into the bathroom and ask her if she'd called the tree guy. The simple answer to this would have been, "No, I'm so sorry, I forgot." Instead, Shelly was angry. This all happened in a split second, as most arguments do, but she was standing there stressed as hell, with her mind elsewhere, and she was mad that Jake was reminding her of something she forgot.

Shelly told me that she got defensive and was nasty to Jake. She said, "You know, I've got so many things to do and I've been busy planning meals for you and the kids while I'm gone and making sure car pool arrangements are made…

blah…blah….blah." She told me later, "Abby, I know now that I got defensive because I was distracted. I was standing there absorbed in my own feelings and busy thoughts and Jake asking about the tree guy put me over the edge!"

As you might imagine, Jake didn't like being yelled at just because he asked a simple question. So, he became defensive and basically retorted, "You don't have to jump down my throat! You do this all the time and I'm sick of it!" When Shelly left on her trip later that day, they were angry at one another and in a bad place.

When Shelly came to talk to me after her business trip, she had done some soul searching and recognized that she had *so* many examples like this. She realized that the majority of their misunderstandings, arguments, frustrations and annoyances were all due to one of them being distracted. Since Jake wasn't willing to come in to therapy (he had told Shelly that their problems were due to her anger issues), we started with Shelly working on consistent self-awareness, so she could stop herself from making this mistake over and over again. Once she started practicing some attention training techniques (tools that literally help you train your attention to be in the present moment), the majority of these issues resolved themselves almost immediately.

In a later session, Shelly said, "I've only been doing this for about six weeks now and already we're getting along 100 percent better. I thought our issue was that we didn't know how to communicate. But our real issue is that we're both lost in our own world half the time so, of course, we were fighting and bugging each other. Now that I'm more self-aware, I catch myself constantly about to say something nasty because I wasn't really listening or paying attention. The issue wasn't that we weren't communicating. The issue was that we weren't really listening to one another because we were distracted!"

The 10 Keys to Being Happily Married

In another session, Shelly told me, "I know it sounds crazy, but I could swear that Jake's more self-aware now, too. It seems like he stops himself more or he'll actually say sorry when he's overreacted or not listened to what I said! That's never happened before. Our relationship really has changed so much. It just feels easier and lighter."

Think about how many times a day you're doing one thing but thinking about another. Learning to train your attention to be in the here and now is incredibly important so you don't have these moments. Learning to check in with yourself so you can *act not react* is what it's all about.

The research backs me up on this. Many studies have shown a high correlation between some kind of attention training or "mindfulness practice" and an improved, more satisfying relationship. Couples report more closeness, better communication and a greater acceptance of one another when one or both of them are involved in some kind of attention training.[17] In fact, even when couples *do* experience conflict, those who utilize attention training say they feel less stressed in those moments, so their fights are shorter and less harmful.[18]

And here's the number one reason why you care about attention training and self-awareness. Is this the first thing you've ever read about how to be in a happy relationship? I'll bet the answer is "no." My guess is you've already learned tools to stop fights, reignite passion or improve communication. But what's happened when you've been in a fight or stressful situation with your partner? Did you remember to use any of the great tools you learned? Probably not.

That's because you forget all the great stuff you've learned and react with the same old responses, words or actions. In the moments when you need those healthy tools the most, *you forget to use them*. You stay stuck in old cycles or patterns because you're distracted and not focused in the present like you need to be.

---

17 *http://www.mindfulnessmalta.com/user_files/2/mindfulness-and-relationships.pdf*
18 *http://greatergood.berkeley.edu/article/item/can_mindfulness_reduce_conflict_in_relationships*

Self-awareness is huge for everyone, but especially when you're in a relationship where your partner isn't open to making changes. Why? Because it feels like your partner is rejecting and abandoning you when they don't make your relationship a priority or when they say you're the one with the problem. It's then too easy to get caught up in resentment, hopelessness and anger. When you bring these three things to the relationship every day, it's not going to improve. In fact, you'll end up in a horrible, downward spiral and the relationship will worsen.

When you have self-awareness, you can see that you're feeling rejected and reacting in an unhealthy way. You can then stop, recalibrate your thinking to a more open and compassionate mindset and change your own behavior. Once you do this, your partner will pick up on these changes (remember that unconscious mind processing 11 million bits per second!) and they'll start acting differently in return.

It's all about your intention. When you have self-awareness, you become aware (and in control) of your intention. We all have an intention before we do or say anything, we just don't generally think of it like that. When your intentions aren't good (whether you realize this or not), your actions follow, and your relationship will feel like a struggle or like it's in a constant downward spiral (we'll talk more about intentions in Chapter Five).

If you intend to be loving and have a loving relationship, then that's what will present itself. You'll see miraculous changes if you start *thinking* differently about your partner consistently—you'll start to feel and see an *upward* spiral.

This isn't just because of some "love is the only answer" platitude, but because when you act and feel loving, you'll feel better! It becomes its own cycle. Just like feeling crappy can become its own cycle (you feel bad, you act negatively to people, people act crappy back, yucky things happen to you or you don't notice the good things because you feel so crappy, blah, blah, blah). Having a loving and compassionate focus has *its* own pattern.

> *You can't make someone love you...but you can love them; you can love yourself and them.*

It's easy to act loving when someone is acting loving back. What's *hard* is to be loving when your partner isn't acting loving toward you. But this is a crucial component to happy and healthy relationships. The other person is often unconsciously testing, "Do you really love me? What if I act like this? What if you see this really crazy side of me?" When you respond from a loving place, you're showing what unconditional love and unconditional acceptance are all about.

Remember, you *feel* the way you *think*. If you want to change your feelings about your partner and your relationship, you have to change those thoughts first. Attention training and self-awareness is the answer for noticing your thoughts, so you can change them and your resultant actions.

When negative thoughts come into your mind, they can run wild and trigger destructive emotions like resentment, fear, depression, hopelessness, hate and anxiety. Mental training of any kind allows you to identify and control your thoughts, which allows you to control your emotions.

Being mindful also allows you to see yourself and your emotions objectively. It creates something called response flexibility, which is basically the ability to pause before you act or respond. It's the ability to act, not react.

Most importantly, mental training, such as meditation, mindfulness and attention training, rewires your brain.

The 10 Keys to Being Happily Married

We'll go more into the research later in this book, but I'd like to give you a couple of key concepts now so you can see how vital it is to learn to be self-aware.

Neuroplasticity is the brain's incredible capacity to change and adapt. It's how the brain physiologically changes itself depending on what you're doing and thinking and how you're interacting with the environment. The brain is dynamic and, from the time it begins to develop in utero until the day you die, it changes and remolds itself in response to your experiences. Your brain is NOT a done deal. The brain rewires and changes, physically, *all the time*. What you focus on creates new neural pathways, new connections in your mind and thoughts. It's said that cells that fire together wire together. Now, the big question is: what are you wiring?

If you cringe when you walk in your house because you're waiting to get yelled at and you do this over and over—this creates a neural pathway or wiring. If you think about how ungrateful, unappreciative and unthoughtful your partner is all the time, this is what gets wired in your brain. If you replay a scene when your partner was negative, critical or nagging over and over again in your mind, then this is what gets wired. If you allow negative thoughts to occupy your brain, this wiring (what we think of as thoughts) becomes more entrenched and stronger.

The good news is that you can flip the script. For example, focusing on something positive, like being *generous* with your partner, will *also* physically change your brain. Richard Davidson, a prominent neuroscience professor at the University of Wisconsin-Madison, has been working with monks who meditate on compassion, love and generosity for many years. He found that these monks had actually altered the structure and function of their brains! His research has shown that "The best way to activate positive-emotion circuits in the brain is through generosity…There are systematic changes in the brain that are associated with acts of generosity."[19]

Imagine training yourself to focus on being compassionate, generous and patient with your partner (and yourself). The more you do it, the more the brain wires itself in this way and the easier it becomes.

Let me give you a totally badass example of wiring your brain purposefully. Dr. Herbert Benson of Harvard University has been studying the "Tum-mo" or "inner fire" monks of Tibet for over 20 years.[20] As a scientist, he became interested in the Buddhist belief that "The reality we live in is not the ultimate one. There's another reality we can tap into that's unaffected by our emotions, by our everyday world." Buddhists believe this state of mind can be achieved by doing good for others and by meditation.

The Tum-mo monks have a ritual where they seclude themselves in an unheated room, in the dead of winter (we're talking freezing temperatures here), high in the Himalayan Mountains. They sit in a meditation posture directly on the concrete floor of the temple while soaking wet sheets are draped over their bodies. Solely through the power of concentration, they thoroughly dry these sheets, right on their bodies! These monks actually raise their body temperature through their meditation so you can see smoke rising from the sheets as they dry in the cold room!

We see this type of "mind over matter" in Western society, too. The "placebo effect" has been heavily researched, and we've seen everything from sugar pills having the same effect as Prozac to people getting drunk off non-alcoholic beer to fake surgeries improving health.

---

19   https://news.wisc.edu/study-shows-compassion-meditation-changes-the-brain/
20   https://news.harvard.edu/gazette/story/2002/04/meditation-changes-temperatures/

The 10 Keys to Being Happily Married

So, when I say that by having a clear intention and consistent focus, you can transform fear and doubt into hope and possibility, I'm serious (and there's research out there to back me up).

ACTION TIPS

At this point, you understand why self-awareness and learning to train your attention where you want it, when you want it, is critical. Now you're ready to take some action.

In my experience, many people are turned off to the idea of self-awareness and attention training because they think they'll need to meditate for an hour a day or something like that. You actually don't need to meditate at all (although that's a great technique, too). There are lots of other tools to learn to stay focused in the here and now. Here are two to get you started:

Tip #1:

Stop and bring yourself to the present moment every time you eat something for the next week.

Tip #2:

Set a reminder on your phone to alert you at three different times during your day (e.g., 9:00am, 1:00pm and 6:00pm). When you hear that reminder, simply notice where your mind was as non-judgmentally as possible (being non-judgmental is often the hardest part).

Gently bring your mind back to focus fully on whatever you're doing. If you're washing the dishes when you hear the alert and you realize that you've been planning the rest of your day, replaying an argument with your partner over and over in your head or thinking about what you want to have for lunch, just bring your attention back to how your hands feel in the warm, soapy water and focus on washing the dish in your hand. This practice will train your brain to pay attention at other times, so, even when there's no alert, you'll begin to notice yourself paying attention in a moment.

For you overachievers, if you like these Action Tips but want *more*, you can download my FREE Bonus Toolkit at *www.abbymedcalf.com/bonustoolkit*

CHAPTER FOUR

KEY #2: THE IMPORTANCE OF ANSWERING BIDS

Now that you're a self-awareness ninja, you're ready for the second key to a long and happy marriage, which is all about something called "bids." Bids are a term coined by marriage researcher John Gottman.[21] They are basically any attempt you or your partner makes to connect. The key is to move toward your partner and "answer" their bid in a positive way (even if they're not doing the same for you).

Your partner has been making bids for a long time, but you probably miss at least half of them. Your partner might comment on a movie they're watching, a bird they saw outside or about something that happened at work. Maybe they ask a question about what you'd like for dinner, or where you'd like to go on vacation or if you'd like to go for a walk. You've likely been tracking these as simple comments or questions that don't mean much. However, they're actually quite important. **Any bid needs your attention**.

---

21   https://www.gottman.com/blog/turn-toward-instead-of-away/

Your partner isn't just mentioning something, they're actually looking for your interest or support, hoping to connect with you about whatever it is they're bringing up. It's generally not a conscious thought to bond, but it's a bid at connection nonetheless.

Think back on conversations you've had with your partner over the last week or two. Think about all the times you thought they were just making an off-hand comment, nagging or mindlessly saying something. That's not the case. *Every time* your partner makes a comment, they're making a bid.

Let me give you a fabulous example from my very own life: My man is really into working out and being physical. He loves it. He says crazy things like, "Oooh, I *get* to go work out." (I know, it seems like he should take medication for this, but the doctor actually says this thinking is healthy!) Right now, he's really into Spartan races.[22] Maybe you've seen these on TV. Men and women run a five- to ten-mile course while crawling through mud, over walls and basically getting through tons of obstacles that most people wouldn't want to attempt unless they were running from a herd of wildebeests.

He recently completed a race and, in the weeks leading up to it, wanted to watch Spartan races on TV and would constantly look at different exercises and courses on the internet. He would often call me over to look at a video of someone jumping over fire or to watch one of the races on TV. Here's the thing: every time he says something like, "This is a cool course," or "Wow! I can't believe how this guy did this," he's not just commenting on the activity. *He's actually making a bid.*

---

[22] http://www.spartan.com/en

I could ignore his comments or nod my head benignly and smile, but these wouldn't be connecting answers to his bids. Instead, I get my butt up and sit next to him while he's watching something. I comment myself on what I'm seeing or ask questions about an exercise or course. In other words, I answer his bid and connect. I go with him to most races, take pictures and get excited for him. I've made little movies of his races, driven him to and from races, flown to other states with him to cheer him on, bought him gear (who knew you could order a spear on Amazon?) and I've filled a bath with ice back at the hotel room (I don't mind telling you that's a lot of trips to the ice machine), so he could cool his sore muscles after a race.

Now, is this something I'm interested in otherwise? No, it's not (I can't even wear my stilettos at these things—barbaric!). However, I really do get excited with him because I'm a "Gary fan," even though I'm not an "obstacle course fan."

Now, don't get me wrong. There are times I just can't watch another race or video. However, I consciously try to make those times the exception, not the rule. No one is perfect (not even me), so this isn't about answering every bid, but it *is* about making them a priority. Gottman calls this "turning toward" instead of "turning away" from the bid and your partner. You have a choice, every time, in how you respond.

If your partner thinks politics, your children, what's for dinner or cats are important enough to bring up, then you need to recognize and respect that. Another, more common, example of this might be when a wife asks a husband what he wants for dinner. Often the husband will say, "I don't care; whatever's easiest for you." This is *not* answering the wife's bid. This is dismissing her feelings and acting like dinner isn't something important, even though the wife might spend *a lot* of time thinking about healthy meals to make, shopping and cooking.

I'm not saying the wife thinks cooking dinner is the most important thing in the world, but it's something that occupies a lot more of her time and head space than most would imagine, and she'd like to be supported and appreciated for that. How you do that isn't just by saying "Thanks for a great meal" or "I really appreciate all the work you put into this" (although that's nice, too). To really answer this bid, you'd need to be part of the planning and process of making dinner. Give a suggestion, "How about chicken tonight? I really like how you did those BBQ drumsticks a few weeks ago." Or maybe you could ask some questions: "What are the choices you've got on hand?"; "Is there anything that feels easiest to you?"; "Do you want me to fire up the grill?" or "Would you rather we went out tonight instead of you cooking?"

The point is to get into a bit of a dialogue about it. It doesn't have to be an hour-long conversation, but stop what you're doing, look up and give your full attention and put some skin in the game. That's it.

Turning away from a bid could look like a lot of things, such as

- Dismissing or ignoring
- Continuing whatever you were doing without stopping (like not looking up from your computer, TV or book)
- Allowing your attention to be diverted easily, such as hearing the ding on your phone and checking your text messages while your partner is talking (note to self: unless you're due for emergency surgery, you can wait five minutes to check your phone)
- Interrupting or changing the subject
- Simply saying "no" as your automatic response

Sometimes, bids are even met with outright hostility, "Why do you keep bugging me about this?" or "Why are you interrupting me while I'm in the middle of making dinner/watching the game/answering emails?"

Gottman says of turning *away* from bids, "These bidding interactions had profound effects on marital well-being. Couples who had divorced after a six-year follow up had 'turn-toward bids' only 33% of the time."[23]

In other words, only three out of every ten bids for emotional connection were met with support, interaction and intimacy. The couples who were still together after six years had "turn-toward bids" 87 percent of the time. In other words, these couples were getting their emotional needs met nine times out of every ten bid attempts.

When marriages are struggling, I hear the same thing over and over: "We don't communicate." This is the place to start. *Having deep conversations when the trust and connection is thin or broken down is not the way to go.* You've got to start with these micro-connections. You've got to start with where the interest *is*, not where you want it to be. Especially if your partner isn't willing to put in any real effort right now.

If your partner doesn't want to work on the relationship, having heavy conversations about it isn't going to help because your partner isn't where you are! Instead of trying to push or control that, **meet your partner where they're at and start with the bids they're making**.

When your partner starts seeing your interest and caring, they start to feel more connected to you. They start to feel like you're on the same team. Once you get to this place

---

23   https://www.gottman.com/blog/an-introduction-to-emotional-bids-and-trust/

consistently, you build trust. If you want to have those deeper conversations, it has to be from a connected and trusting place in the relationship.

REAL-LIFE EXAMPLE:

I worked with a woman we'll call Colleen. Her husband, Santiago, LOVED soccer. He had played as a kid in Argentina, watched all the soccer he could on TV, played in two different soccer leagues (it *was* three, but Colleen put her foot down on that one) and he coached a kids' soccer team that both his daughters played for.

Colleen came to me ready to get rid of Santiago: "All he cares about is soccer: soccer with his friends, for himself or with the girls. I'm sick of it. He never wants to do anything with me, and I've asked over and over for him to make us a date night or something. He'll do all this planning for his teams, but nothing for us. He won't even come into therapy to talk about all this."

I told her to start answering his bids and to figure out ways she could support the soccer without feeling like it was taking over her own life. She resisted this idea at first, saying, "That's just going to make it even worse if I pay attention to the soccer!" I assured her it was worth a try and not to be afraid to answer any bids he was making.

Colleen came into her next session already amazed. "First of all, I didn't realize how often he makes bids that I was ignoring or even getting mad about!"

She told me how she soon saw that Santiago would often try to connect first thing in the morning when he had a lot of energy: "I didn't realize that he was trying to speak to me in the mornings because I was always so focused on the girls and getting them ready and out the door on time." Colleen often waited until the very last second to wake up in the mornings and then rushed around like crazy, with no time for Santiago (or herself).

The 10 Keys to Being Happily Married

To correct this, Colleen started getting up 15 minutes earlier (eventually it even became 30 minutes earlier) so she could focus more on Santiago (and herself) in the mornings: "I can't believe what a difference that little bit of time makes. I used to think there was no way I could get up earlier, that sleep was the most important thing. Now I know my relationship is the most important thing and giving up a little sleep is so worth it!"

Colleen and Santiago started having small connections and conversations in the mornings that were light and loving. Without all the rushing, Colleen started to really focus on Santiago and what he was saying. She realized that he was often trying to get her engaged in a conversation (and not just about soccer), but she was blowing him off. Then, later, she'd try to have these conversations when Santiago was preoccupied with other things and he'd blow her off. Someone had to stop this relationship gridlock and be the first to make a move, and it was Colleen.

After just two months, she came in and said, "I'm loving these morning times with Santiago. We hang out and drink coffee just for 10 or 15 minutes, but it's so nice. Both of us are fresh and it's a great way to start the day. I feel better about him for the rest of the day and have better thoughts because of this great start every morning. We've even had sex in the morning twice!"

Colleen also started to focus more on making sure Santiago's soccer clothes were clean and put back in his bag for practices, that she packed snacks for him to take with him and even went to a few games (something she hadn't done in years).

In another session, she told me, "I can't believe the turnaround in him and never would have believed this would work! He's more attentive and he's actually asking *me* questions about *my* life! I was worried that focusing more on soccer would make it even bigger, but it did the opposite. He actually stopped watching a game the other night to sit and talk with me! It's not perfect, and I'd still like to see less focus on soccer, but it's so much better and I didn't really need to do much but change my head about all this."

This is what happens when we start to show an active interest in what's important to our partner. They feel seen and appreciated and, in turn, want to connect with us.

ACTION TIPS

Tip #1:

You'll notice that staying in the here and now and not allowing yourself to get distracted is the best way to ensure that you're aware when bids are made so you can turn toward them instead of turning away. If you haven't done one of the Action Tips from Key #1, Self-Awareness, choose one now to start doing. If you've already been doing one of the tips, continue to practice so these tools become habits.

Tip #2:

Make a commitment to say "yes" to *whatever* your partner asks for the next week. Any bid they make, jump in with enthusiasm. It might be a walk, watching something on TV together, a blow job or helping with dinner, but, whatever it is, just say "Yes!" You'll notice more intimacy and connection right away.

For you overachievers, if you like these Action Tips but want *more*, you can download my FREE Bonus Toolkit at *www.abbymedcalf.com/bonustoolkit*

CHAPTER FIVE

KEY #3: SET AN INTENTION OF KINDNESS

How your relationship feels day to day boils down to what energy, attitude and thoughts you're bringing *to* the relationship. Are you focusing on being kind, generous, open, loving and patient? Or are you generally bringing criticism, hostility, contempt or negativity?

Research[24] has shown that kindness (along with emotional stability) is the most important predictor of satisfaction and stability in a marriage. Kindness makes each partner feel cared for, understood and validated. Kindness makes people feel loved.

If you're spending time focusing on all the things wrong with your partner, you'll start to see the negative everywhere. Essentially, you'll start proving yourself right. This happens because of a little-known, but very important, part of your brain circuitry called your reticular activating system, or RAS for short.[25]

---

24   http://www.theatlantic.com/health/archive/2014/06/happily-ever-after/372573/
25   https://www.youtube.com/watch?v=XjL7nliUTz4

Your RAS is like a filter between your conscious and subconscious minds. It takes instructions from your conscious mind and passes them on to your subconscious. You're constantly giving your RAS instructions by what you're thinking about—the problem is that you don't even realize it. If you're thinking, "My partner is always judging and criticizing me," the RAS hears this as the *instruction or order*: "look for my partner criticizing me." Sure enough, your partner is "always" criticizing—you hear it constantly. The RAS is one of the reasons why you'll suddenly notice a lot of pregnant women when you're pregnant or the amount of Nissan Pathfinders on the road after you buy one.

If you're thinking, "If she'd only stop nagging me every day, I could breathe and get to everything on my list," or "If he'd only stop drinking so much, we'd be great," or "The only problem in our relationship is his anger," you're essentially telling that RAS to look for nagging, drinking and anger and it will find it…. OFTEN!

Researchers[26] have found that the couples who look for things to appreciate are happier and stay married longer than those who are always looking for their partner's mistakes. The best way to be appreciative and focus on the positive is to keep it simple and just focus on being kind.

> Kindness should be bottled as Couples' Glue.

The research shows that it creates all the things you're looking for: affection, bonding, validation and *more kindness* as your partner reacts, well, in kind (pun intended).[27]

---

26 *http://www.apa.org/pubs/journals/cfp/*
27 *http://www.pnas.org/content/107/12/5334.abstract*

Open doors, say "please" and "thank you," go out of your way to do something nice for your partner, fold the laundry even when it's not "your turn," you get the idea. *Be kind early and often.* You can do things like buy her flowers or small gifts, give him a blow job (there's no research I could find on this specifically, but in my experience it's 100 percent effective for creating a good mood in my man) or rub your partner's feet. I also want you to just think kind thoughts day to day and weave kindness into the fabric of your interactions with your partner.

One way you can be kind is to assume the best in your partner. Your husband isn't deliberately trying to annoy you if he walks by the overflowing garbage can; your wife didn't deliberately forget to pick up your dry cleaning and your partner really didn't see the dog poop in the living room and purposefully leave it for you to clean up (OK, that's a stretch, but you get where I'm going here).

One of my clients talks about focusing on having "the most generous interpretation of life events." I love this. Cashier at the grocery store rude and short? Think that maybe he's having a hard day and hates his job. Driver in front of you cut you off? Think that maybe she didn't see your car and how we all make mistakes (I, myself, have accidentally cut off other drivers because I didn't see them). Your partner comes home in a bad mood? Think that they must have had a hard day and need extra love and compassion.

If your partner says something to you that you don't like, take a moment and try to give the most generous interpretation. In other words, give them the benefit of the doubt *first*. Maybe you could think, "Well, my husband has never been the most thoughtful guy, but he does show me he loves me by how hard he works to provide for me and the kids." Or "I don't love that my wife told me I didn't clean the counter right, but I've got to remember that she's worried

The 10 Keys to Being Happily Married

about her mom, and she gets controlling when she's feeling frightened."

Assume your partner is always doing their best with the tools they have at the time. Even when they screw up, it likely wasn't intended to be all bad, so show some grace, give them a break, and appreciate whatever good intent was at the bottom of whatever happened.

Intentions happen all the time, usually unconsciously. *Setting* intention is literally the opposite. It's having your intentions or your thoughts *consciously* directed toward a desired outcome.

Merriam-Webster dictionary defines an intention as "the thing that you plan to do or achieve: an aim or purpose." This simple definition is perfect because it outlines what intentions really do, at their very core: they give you a target and something to shoot for.

I define intention as a guiding principle for how you want to be, live and show up in the world. It's a way to bring your heart and mind into alignment.

I don't want you to confuse intentions with goals. You don't want to attach an expectation to your intention. Unlike goals, intentions often aren't tangible. Get that promotion, put money in retirement every month, and lose 10 pounds are all goals. You will evaluate and measure these goals. You don't do that with intentions.

To set an intention, you really just want to ask yourself: "How do I want to feel in my relationship?" You can use this answer to set your intention. Then, you'll reflect back to your partner what you want.

Examples of intention would go something like this: "It's my intention to

- Be patient and kind in all my interactions today."

- Listen attentively when my partner speaks to me."
- Be responsible and trustworthy."
- Only speak when I need to."
- Find fun and laughter in my relationship today."
- Be compassionate with my partner today."
- Notice my partner's mood."
- Practice active listening in all my interactions today."
- Notice what I'm feeling before I speak."
- Pay attention to the answers people give me."
- Be generous with my partner."

Keep your intentions simple and as short as possible so you can remind yourself of them often. You can set multiple intentions, but it's best to set only one or two per day.

REAL-LIFE EXAMPLE

When Jeannine came to me, she spent the first hour just complaining about her husband, Mike. Every time I told her it wasn't going to be helpful to use the time complaining, she would say, "Oh yes, you're right." But, within minutes, she was back to blaming and criticizing.

It was clear that thinking negatively about Mike had become a long-standing habit and she wasn't even aware that she was doing it constantly. We worked on self-awareness together so that she could notice when she was doing this and shift her focus. She started setting daily intentions to be kind, gracious and patient.

Gradually, Jeannine started to be more aware of just how often she was looking at her husband's faults (which, by her admission, was pretty much all the time). She started to focus, daily, on being kind to him and trying to see what he was doing well. In the beginning, the only good thing she could think of was the fact that he went to work every day to financially support the family.

However, over time, she started to notice many more things he did that were good or great: often complimenting her and thanking her for making dinner, always leaving the toilet seat down (she didn't appreciate this until one of her other friends was complaining about how her husband always left the toilet seat up!), how great a dad he was to their daughter and giving her the parking space in the garage so it was safer and easier for her to get in and out of the house.

In just a month's time, Jeannine came into session in a great mood. She said, "Once I started changing my mindset from focusing on the negative to being kind, all sorts of things started popping up. I started thanking him for the things he was doing and we started getting along better. He started listening more to me and asking if he could help. We started laughing more. Things just started snowballing in a great direction—all because I was setting this intention to be nicer every day."

But, the best part was how she started feeling day to day: "I think I was depressed before and now I feel happier. I still want my marriage to improve, but I feel hope and that's making me feel happier. I've even had two people tell me I looked younger, and I think it's this work I'm doing!"

Setting an intention of kindness is a way to know, every day, that you're doing your part to make the relationship better. No matter what comes at you, you can feel more confident that your side of the street is clean. It's never a mistake to be kind to your partner. If you want a loving relationship, you can't be stuck in fear and negativity. Those things never add up to love. Kindness is an awesome place to start any loving relationship.

Wayne Dyer said, "Our intention creates our reality" and the Buddha said, "The mind is everything. What you think, you become." Focus on what you're thinking about and set an intention to be kind to your partner today.

ACTION TIPS

Tip #1:

It's important to give your partner and family the best of yourself, not the dregs of what's left over after a long workday. Walking in the door and saying, "Hi Honey, how was your day?" gets you crappy results like "good" or "fine." You're on autopilot and you're not going to have the best and healthiest interactions this way. This is another way we get into fights, have misunderstandings and feel disconnected.

Setting intention before we interact helps create immediate connection. Setting intention means you're going to actively and consciously think of how you want to be with your partner. You can set an intention to be open, patient, fun, curious or whatever floats your boat. But the very best intention is to be kind.[28]

> My clients report that setting intention consistently is one of the single most effective tools I've ever given them.

Make a commitment to set an intention daily before you walk in your house. Every time you get to your door, stop, set a conscious intention and then walk in. If you're home and you hear your partner entering the house, do the same. Stop and consciously set an intention before you greet them. The more often you set intention, the better your life will be.

---

[28] http://www.abbymedcalf.com/learn-to-set-intention-with-this-1-minute-video/

If you're practicing the mindful/self-awareness tips from Chapter One, you can set intention every time your mindfulness reminder alert goes off in the day. You can remember what to do with the acronym **SINGS**. You're going to

- **S**top whatever you're doing
- **I**nhale and exhale consciously for one breath
- **N**otice where your mind was and what you were thinking about
- **G**ently bring your attention back to the present
- **S**et an intention for how you'd like to be moving forward in your day.

Tip #2:

Remember the RAS I talked about earlier? You can *deliberately* program the RAS by thoughtfully *choosing* the exact messages you send. If you really want to find fulfillment, happiness and connection with your partner, you need to shift what you're focusing on and be conscious of the orders you're giving to your RAS.

To do this, text your partner one thing you're grateful for about them every day, for one week. If you don't want to text them, start keeping a journal about what you appreciate about your partner. Write something in it, every day for (at least) one week.

For you overachievers, if you like these Action Tips but want *more*, you can download my FREE Bonus Toolkit at *www.abbymedcalf.com/bonustoolkit*

CHAPTER SIX

KEY #4: BE VULNERABLE (IT'S NOT AS SCARY AS YOU THINK)

When most people (including myself) hear the word vulnerability, their first reaction is, "I'll pass, but thanks for asking." I wish it could be that simple, but to have an emotionally close relationship, you've got to have yourself some vulnerability. Vulnerability is a cornerstone for any intimate relationship. Being vulnerable means your partner can see and reach you; they can access the real you.

Without vulnerability, trust diminishes or becomes nonexistent. Some people think of trust as black and white: you either trust someone or you don't. But trust is really along a continuum. There are many shades and grades of trust. You might trust your partner with money or not to cheat on you, but do you trust them with your heart? Do you share the difficult parts of yourself? Do you show them your soft underbelly, or do you think they'll use this information against you or throw it back in your face in an argument?

Without trust, true emotional closeness or intimacy is impossible. And this is where it all falls apart because, when intimacy is off the table, all you have left is that daily grind of commitment: bills, car pools, farting, towels left on the floor and sitting down to meals. Without commitment…. well, you can see where this is going.

As I said earlier, vulnerability is one of those words most people don't like to hear at first blush. I thought for most of my life that being vulnerable meant being exposed, which would open me to hurt, rejection and humiliation. So, I avoided it at all costs and my guess is that you're doing (or have done) the same. Eleanor Roosevelt taught us many years ago that no one can make us feel inferior without our consent, but too often we can forget this lesson and put our self-esteem in other people's hands. We tend to be very susceptible to others' opinions of us, especially our partner, who can hurt us like no other.

One of the hardest things about vulnerability is managing all the (emotional) uncertainty. Most of us like to be in control (I'm a control enthusiast myself). Allowing ourselves to be vulnerable means we're giving up control: "What will my partner think?"; "Will they still want to be with me when they know about this?"; "Will they now see me as weak and take advantage of me?"

We try to outrun vulnerability with control, making things as definite and certain as we can. The problem is that this is all fear-based thinking, and *you can't have a love relationship based on fear*. Vulnerability leads to trust, openness, belonging, confidence, connection and happiness. These are all the love-based emotions.

Brené Brown, the queen of vulnerability says, "The difficult thing is that vulnerability is the first thing I look for in you and the last thing I'm willing to show you. In you, it's courage and daring. In me, it's weakness."[29] This is an unconscious pattern so many of us are stuck in. Just realizing how much we like it and feel bonded when others are vulnerable can sometimes be enough motivation to get at least a little vulnerable ourselves.

Brené Brown called her seminal book on vulnerability *Daring Greatly*. Do you know why? The phrase is actually from Theodore Roosevelt's "Citizen in a Republic" speech (also known as "The Man in the Arena" speech) that he delivered at the Sorbonne in Paris, France, in 1910.[30] This is the passage that made the speech famous:

> "It's not the critic who counts; not the man who points out how the strong man stumbles or where the doer of deeds could have done them better.
> The credit belongs to the man who is actually in the arena, whose face is marred by dust and sweat and blood; who strives valiantly... who at best knows the triumph of high achievement and who at the worst, if he fails, at least fails while daring greatly."

Vulnerability isn't about being the victor or the loser. It's understanding that both are necessary. It's about being ac-

---

[29] https://www.forbes.com/sites/danschawbel/2013/04/21/brene-brown-how-vulnerability-can-make-our-lives-better/

[30] https://www.scribd.com/document/36660224/The-Man-in-the-Arena-April-23-1910-Theodore-Roosevelt-Speeches-Rooseve

tively and courageously engaged in your life. *It's about being all in.*

It's time to give up on the idea that you need to guard your heart. You can't be fully intimate with your partner if you're guarded. It's time to give up the idea that anyone else, even your partner, can truly hurt you. It's time to take responsibility and be brave in your approach to your life and relationship. This means, it's time to be *relentlessly vulnerable*.

> The secret no one tells you about being vulnerable is that it's not about being exposed: it's about being accessible.

The dictionary definition for accessible is: able to be reached and approachable. Isn't this how you *have* to be in your relationship? Your partner needs to be able to reach you! And you need to be able to reach them.

When you're open and show your true self, your partner can access and connect with you. They can really get to know you. You can have true intimacy—true emotional closeness in your relationship, including the most important relationship of all: the one you have with yourself.

When you let what's on the inside show on the outside, your partner will be drawn to you, just as you're drawn to your partner when they show you who they really are and let you in.

REAL-LIFE EXAMPLE

My client Jack said he couldn't be vulnerable because his strong-willed wife, Amy, would walk all over him. So, he created what he called his "boundaries." "If I don't have these clear boundaries set up, she'll mow right over me. So, I tell her when I'll be home and it's non-negotiable. I have a rule that she can't talk about her work with me (or that's *all* we talk about), and no talks after 7:00pm. I bike ride every Saturday morning until noon, no matter what, and it's up to her to initiate sex because I've been shot down too many times and I'm sick of it."

When Jack came to me to do individual work, it was obvious that he was blaming so much of his unhappiness on his wife and marriage. I'm sure as you read what he said to me, you could feel his frustration, exasperation and annoyance.

I explained to Jack that what he thought were boundaries were really walls. When we feel a need to be this rigid, it's because we're afraid. As I've said, if fear is driving your relationship, you're in trouble! He kept insisting in his sessions that he didn't trust Amy to keep the boundaries but, really, this wasn't about his wife. This was about Jack not trusting *himself* to hold his *own* boundaries.

It's not up to your partner to keep your boundaries—it's up to you to accept nothing less. In our work together, I wasn't surprised to find out that Jack grew up with a father who trampled his boundaries at every turn (he actually became a CPA instead of going into psychology because his father refused to pay for college for anything else). Jack ended up blaming his father for his unfulfilling career (and many other things in his life) and then set himself up in a marriage with the same dynamic.

Over the next couple of months, we worked on Jack's self-esteem and confidence. He started to figure out what his boundaries really were (not just rules and walls), and what he really needed to feel loved and respected. The big breakthrough was that he started to hold his boundaries firmly. He started to realize that he was afraid to ask for what he really wanted. He was afraid to be vulnerable and show his true wants and needs because he was afraid of being rejected. He was afraid Amy wouldn't meet him and then where would he be?

In the beginning, Amy pushed back and tried to run over these boundaries (as I predicted she would), but Jack held firm the majority of the time and things started to really change in his home. "It's suddenly like she respects me," he said after seeing me for a little over three months. "It's like the more I stick to my boundaries, the more she likes and trusts me. We're getting along so much better and her intensity level has gone down about 24 notches!"

In another session, he said, "Since I've been asking for what I want, she started doing it, too. She's being vulnerable with me! She's sharing how she's been scared of losing me. I had all those rules, that I thought were boundaries, and she felt far from me. *I was sooooo not vulnerable.* I was all closed off. Now that I'm open, she's open. I can't believe how close I feel to her. I didn't think it was possible."

This is how people react to true boundaries. It's clear where we stand all the time, so we start to feel safe and build trust with our partners (and ourselves). Amy was reacting to Jack's fear. She could feel it and it made her unconsciously anxious and uncomfortable, so she became more controlling. When she got those clear boundaries and limits from Jack, she could relax and trust him more.

Amy changed because Jack changed.

Abby Medcalf

Being vulnerable and saying what you really want from a loving place, then sticking to your boundaries, is another way you can change your relationship, even if your partner won't do a thing.

ACTION TIPS

Tip #1:

Set an intention to be vulnerable with your partner every day for two weeks. You don't even need to know what this looks like. Your subconscious will pick up on the message and do the work for you.

Tip #2:

Asking for help or admitting when you've made a mistake are two great ways of being vulnerable. These are skills that you likely haven't learned, as many of us are taught that making mistakes or asking for help is bad and shows weakness. Start changing this attitude by practicing these two skills with friends. Tell a friend one thing you messed up or ask for help from one of your friends, once a day, for the next week.

For you overachievers, if you like these Action Tips but want *more*, you can download my FREE Bonus Toolkit at *www.abbymedcalf.com/bonustoolkit*

CHAPTER SEVEN

KEY #5: YOUR LIZARD BRAIN AND WHY YOU NEED TO SAY "YES" FIRST

This marks the halfway point in this book. First, I want to say "congratulations" for getting this far. Second, I want to say, "Do your homework!!" I know that so many of you reading this have *not* practiced the Action Tips consistently (I see you!). I said it at the beginning and I'll say it again, you've got to practice these new behaviors, or they won't become habits and you'll just end up sliding back into old, negative patterns. I don't want that to happen to you!

OK, I'm done with my I'm-a-Jewish-Mother-who-wants-to-control-you rant and now it's time to get into one of my favorite keys to change your relationship, even if your partner won't do a thing. To understand this key, you've got to first understand some things about how your brain works, so we're going to start with a little biology. But don't worry, I make it super understandable and usable!

Your brain has been evolving for many more years than you likely realize. No matter where you start: 200 million years ago, with the first mammals or 200,000 years ago when homo sapiens made their first appearance, the human brain has been evolving for a looooonnnnngggg time.

The problem is that, in the big picture of life on this planet, we're just blips. We're talking about a universe that's 3.5 billion years old (give or take a few hundred million years). Humans just haven't been around that long and the brain you're dealing with today is adapted to a world from more than a million years ago: back when it was rare to meet someone you didn't know (and dangerous usually if you did), when food, shelter and water were scarce and when there were no McDonalds, no antibiotics, and no police or internet.

To survive, our ancestors focused on what author Rick Hanson[31] calls carrots and sticks. Carrots were the good things that we wanted (like food and sex), and sticks were the threats that we needed to avoid (like animals trying to kill us). If you missed a carrot, it wasn't great, but another bunny would likely be hopping by soon to kill and eat.

However, if you missed a stick way back when, you were dead. That was it. Lights out. You were never going to have a chance to look for a carrot again! So, as humans, we evolved to be WAY more focused on avoiding sticks than getting carrots. This is what happens to you in your relationship. Doing things to improve the relationship and looking for ways your partner is awesome (looking for carrots) is *way less* motivating than looking for ways your partner messed up (looking for those sticks).

And there's another subtle piece to this. We've evolved to be on the lookout for those sticks *all the time*. Sometimes our

---

31 https://www.amazon.com/Hardwiring-Happiness-Science-Contentment-Confidence/dp/0385347332/ref=sr_1_1?ie=UTF8&qid=1535487213&sr=8-1&keywords=hardwiring+the+brain+for+happiness&dpID=41t4M8kSA3L&preST=_SY344_BO1,204,203,200_QL70_&dpSrc=srch

ancestors would be afraid that a tiger was going to jump out, but no tiger was actually there. However, other times they'd be afraid a tiger would jump out and a tiger *would* be there. Because of this, your brain is trained to *always* look for the tiger because if you missed it, you were dead.

You've evolved to look for any way your partner might jump out at you. You train yourself to look for them messing up, cheating, lying, chewing with their mouth open, being late, leaving a dish on the counter, not making the bed correctly or any number of other things that your brain perceives as a threat.

Since it was life and death to pay more attention to sticks than carrots, to look around every corner for that tiger, our brains developed a *negativity bias*. Let me give you a quick example you can probably relate to.

Not too long ago, I conducted a workshop in Texas. There were about 300 people there and, at the end, I asked the participants to complete feedback evaluations, so I could improve my future workshops. Of the roughly 300 people in the room, 177 completed the questionnaire. Of the 177 who completed the form, 152 people rated my talk as excellent. Most said it was the best they'd ever been to and heaped praise onto little old me. Another 21 rated it "very good" and also had excellent feedback.

However, four people absolutely hated me. I don't mean they didn't think it was great—I mean they just didn't like *me*. One went on and on about how Jews are racist, so I shouldn't be able to speak in front of others and another thought it was "highly inappropriate" that I was wearing high heels to give a lecture. The other two just thought I sucked and my information was bad, stupid and not very well-thought-out. So, although the VAST majority of the audience thought I was a rock star and couldn't wait to hear me speak again, and even though some of the negative feedback was clearly skewed and unreasonable (and at least racist and sexist), where do you think I focused? Which evaluations do you think I read again and again and talked to other people about?

We're all hardwired to do this. In fact, your brain reacts more intensely to negative emotions and events than positive ones, so you'll always remember that negative feedback first. As if that wasn't enough, *negative events are recognized and processed more quickly and easily than positive ones in your brain.* Oy!

Let me bring this home for you. Let's say you're speaking to your partner in the morning and they seem tense. You ask them what's wrong. They respond, "I've got to run to work and I'm going to be very busy today, but I *am* upset about something. Let's talk when I get home tonight."

When your partner said this, it activated a part of your brain called your amygdala because your brain processed this statement as, *a tiger coming to eat you*. Your amygdala is your brain's watchman and it's always on patrol for any would-be threat.

The amygdala is located in the limbic system, and it's in charge of things like fear and aggression. This is the most ancient part of your brain and its primary job is to keep you safe. It's on the constant lookout for danger (like a tiger that's about to leap out at you or the toilet seat being left in the wrong position). The limbic system is also called the reptilian brain because it's the part of our brain that we share with all reptiles.

Your brain processes your partner's statement, "Let's talk when I get home tonight" as a *big* threat! So, your amygdala starts ringing alarm bells, which lights up your sympathetic nervous system and your fight, flight or freeze response. Next, a bunch of stress hormones such as adrenaline, cortisol and norepinephrine come flooding into your system.

You know that "sinking feeling" you get when it feels like your stomach has dropped out? Well, that's actually the blood rushing to your legs to RUN from the tiger! Rationally, you know there's no tiger, but your brain is *not* acting from its rational real estate at this point.

Your heart starts beating faster (because your brain thinks you're about to start running from the tiger), your thoughts speed up and you feel totally anxious, nervous and distraught (you are about to be eaten, after all). Maybe you sweat when you get upset. This is to cool you off as you run and also so that your skin is slick for when that tiger tries to get you—maybe his teeth will slide off! All of these "automatic" responses happen because your outdated hardwiring takes over as it prepares to run from that tiger.

Over time, negative experiences make the amygdala even more sensitive. So, you'll likely have the experience of your partner upsetting you more and more often and even when they don't do anything that "big" or consequential. Just about "any little thing" can set you off. Sound familiar?

To make matters worse, remember that cortisol I just mentioned that's now whipping around your brain? Well, it overstimulates and weakens a part of your brain called the hippocampus. Enough cortisol, over a long enough period of time, will actually *shrink* your hippocampus. This is a big problem, because the hippocampus is the part of the brain that helps you be realistic and put things into perspective (because it calms the amygdala and tells the brain to chill out). If it's shrinking, it can't do its job. Now it's harder to put that fight with your partner into perspective *and* harder to stay calm. Again, sound familiar?

Because of this crazed amygdala and your negativity bias, your brain tends to *over*estimate threats and *under*estimate your resources and opportunities and general good stuff in your world.

The 10 Keys to Being Happily Married

> In the end, your negativity bias pulls your attention toward anything bad that happens with your partner and then makes you overreact to it!

As if that's not bad enough, it also *minimizes* anything positive. As a result, you won't notice the good stuff that happens or, if you do happen to see it, your brain tells you to *under*react. Your negativity bias is great for survival but not so great for having a connected, peaceful and fulfilling relationship.

Let's take a minute and talk a little more about that amygdala and your fight, flight or freeze response (the science portion of this book is almost over, so please hang in there if this stuff bores you). I want you to imagine yourself walking in the woods and you come upon a snake (yikes). There are just three things that snake will do. It'll attack you (fight), it'll slither away (flee) or it'll stay still and hope the danger (you) passes without seeing it (freeze).

Now, imagine yourself walking into the house and your partner is angry with you about something. You can feel their outrage coming off of them in waves. Your brain thinks this is one of those tigers, so your amygdala lights up and you're left with only three things to do. You'll attack your partner (fight). You'll find a way to get the heck out of there (flee). Or, you'll say nothing or agree to anything they say ("Yes, Dear") in hopes that the danger will pass (freeze).

> Every time you focus on your own, or someone else's, weaknesses, limitations or what's wrong, it reinforces fear, which keeps your amygdala lit up.

I bet this has happened to you. You start thinking of something your partner did that pissed you off and it just makes you angrier and angrier. Then you start thinking of *all* the other annoying things your partner has done and it's all you can think about. Before you know it, it seems like annoying things are *all* they do.

When you get stuck in these repetitive cycles of negativity with your partner (or your sister or boss for that matter), you keep your amygdala activated, so your brain basically gets hijacked. *When your limbic system is turned on, you can't reason, think things through or hear suggestions.* Brain imaging has shown that when the amygdala is activated by negative emotions, it actually interferes with the brain's ability to solve problems (or figure out how to get unstuck). This is why, when you're in an argument, you can't remember all the great tools you learned in therapy or in that fantastic book you read!

> What you want to do is switch from your amygdala (reptile brain) to another part of your brain called the prefrontal cortex.

The prefrontal cortex is where your problem-solving, rational thinking, long-term planning, values and judgment all live. When you're operating from your prefrontal cortex, you can be appreciative, have gratitude, find compassion, feel warmth and get creative. You can effectively think of solutions and problem-solve because you can remember all those great relationship tools you learned *and use them!*

Stress of any kind sends your lizard brain into action. It can happen with any number of "stressful" emotions or situations. Every person is different, but the most likely culprits are depression, anxiety, loneliness, overwhelming feelings, sadness, helplessness, hopelessness, rage, jealousy, annoyance, resentment, impatience and frustration. Had any of those lately? Yeah, I thought so.

This means that your lizard brain has been front and center more than you want or likely realize. Think about all the negative patterns you have with your partner. How many times do you have the same argument, the same annoyances, the same frustrations?

How many times have you been annoyed that she left the cap off the toothpaste (again), or angry that he didn't offer to help you bring in the groceries, or felt stressed that she spent too much money, or disappointed when he didn't look up from his cell phone when you asked a question? Every time you face one of these challenges, your amygdala lights up.

Compounding all this negativity bias in your brain is something called neuroplasticity. Neuroplasticity is the brain's ability to physically change, depending on what you do or think about consistently. **Your brain is actually designed to change with what you experience**.[32] What?!?!? Yes, whatever you *repeatedly* experience changes the actual physical structure and neural pathways in your brain. So, whatever you repeatedly think about, feel or want slowly changes your brain and you become hardwired in these ways.

The word "repeatedly" is important. If you think about something briefly and occasionally, that experience simply "comes and goes" in your brain and no strong neural path-

---

[32] https://www.amazon.com/Train-Your-Mind-Change-Brain/dp/0345479890/ref=sr_1_1?s=books&ie=UTF8&qid=1535487445&sr=1-1&keywords=train+your+mind+change+your+brain+by+sharon+begley&dpID=51tftVHELZL&preST=_SY344_BO1,204,203,200_QL70_&dpSrc=srch

ways are laid down. However, when you think about or do something over and over, it becomes entrenched in your neural circuitry and creates new pathways and foundations. Your brain starts to wire itself depending on what you're repeatedly thinking about and doing. Connections you *don't use* shrivel and fade away.

Think of a walking through a field thick with weeds, bushes and grass. If you were to move through it once, not much would happen. But, if you used the same path over and over, it would become worn down over time. In this way, mental states (what you experience in a moment) become neural traits (hardwiring in your brain). Day after day, what you're thinking about is building and changing your brain.

There have been many studies showing how our brains are physically changed by what we think about and focus on. One of the most famous is a study that looked at the brains of London taxi drivers.[33] These drivers have to memorize over 25,000 streets and thousands of landmarks. The study found that these drivers' brains had thickened layers in their hippocampus, the part of the brain that helps with visual spatial memories.

But, maybe that's just when you're learning something. What happens when you just think about something a bunch? Research by neuroscientist Richard Davidson[34] (who I mentioned earlier in this book) found that monks who meditate on compassion have enlarged areas of their brains called the neocortex. This is the part of the brain where we think compassion, gratitude and appreciation live. So, even just thinking about something and not "doing" anything can change the brain.

---

33 *https://www.cell.com/current-biology/fulltext/S0960-9822(11)01267-X*
34 https://www.theatlantic.com/health/archive/2015/07/dalai-lama-neuroscience-compassion/397706/

The 10 Keys to Being Happily Married

It's also been found that, not only do these experiences change the brain, but they actually change how our genes express and operate. For example, if you become a regular meditator, you'll increase the activity of genes that calm stress reactions.

> What all the research tells us is that your experiences matter. What you think about a lot matters.

If you keep thinking self-critically, worrying or complaining, and continually focus on feelings of helplessness, hurt, stress or rage, you're going to change your brain for the worse. Your brain will change and it'll be more reactive; you'll be more vulnerable to anxiety and/or a depressed mood, and you'll be more inclined to feel sad, negative, angry and guilty and to only see the bad everywhere you look.

So, what can I do, Abby?!

By now, you're likely asking, "How do I move from my scared and negative reptilian brain to my resourceful, rational brain?" I've actually got an amazing tool for this—I call it "Say Yes First."

The "Say Yes First" tool helps the brain transition from this fear-based amygdala to the rational prefrontal cortex, so you can have a connected, logical and thoughtful conversation.

The Say Yes First tool is this: you're going to empathize with whatever your partner is saying and match their emotion, but not their tone, and *not* make any suggestions or give any advice.

Let me explain with an example: Let's say your partner is complaining that a coworker is completely horrible and driving them crazy. You listen and then start to come up with awesome suggestions: "Do you really need to even talk to this guy?"; "Why don't you just leave the room whenever he walks in?" or "Have you told your boss about what he's doing?"

Your partner replies with how they've tried "everything." Or they have reasons why none of your ideas will work. They start to get more upset and a little defensive, so you start getting frustrated and say something like, "Well, if you don't want to take any suggestions, why are we talking about this?" The next thing you know, you and your partner are fighting, and you're bewildered. How did we get here?! Why are you pissed at me instead of at the guy from work?! Sound familiar?

When your partner is upset about that guy from work, they're actually thinking he's a tiger about to eat them. *They're in fight, flight or freeze mode so they're NOT able to problem-solve.* When you jump into problem-solving or discussion too soon or say things that you think will comfort your partner like, "It'll be OK, don't worry about this jerk," your partner thinks you don't see the tiger! Your partner thinks you're an idiot who doesn't realize this VERY REAL danger! So your partner escalates until you get the idea.

Your partner is screaming, "There's a tiger coming!!" so if you keep trying to calm or placate them, your partner will just continue to escalate. If you try to problem-solve (Should we run from the tiger? Yell for help? Climb that tree? Tell me your thoughts…), your partner thinks you're insane and not realizing the urgency here and, again, will fight you, flee from you or freeze.

To get out of this cycle, you need to get your partner from their lizard (fight, flight or freeze) brain to their rational, problem-solving prefrontal cortex. To do this, you "Say Yes First." In this situation with your partner complaining about their coworker, I want you to see their side of things as best you can and try to really listen. Then your job is to empathize (say "yes") and say something like, "Darn that sucks. I'm sorry you're dealing with this." You're now building rapport—showing your partner that you're on the same page as them.

By saying "yes" first and empathizing with your partner's feelings, you're essentially saying that you see the tiger! By doing that, it calms your partner because their brain is telling them, "Someone else sees the tiger, too—I have help!"

After you've empathized and said yes first, you can say something like, "Given how things are going with this guy, what do you think your next move could be?" It's likely there will actually be some openness to problem-solving now. At the very least, the energy will come down as your partner feels like you're listening.

One of the little secrets here is that **I want you to match their emotion, but not their tone**. In other words, I want you to see that your partner's upset and try to feel their feelings a bit. So, when you're "saying yes," you need to match whatever emotion they're having. But, you don't want to match their tone, meaning, you don't want to yell or escalate even if they are. So, it's "Man, this sucks. I hate that this guy is still bugging you" *not* "THIS IS TERRIBLE! CRAP! WHAT THE HELL ARE YOU GOING TO DO?!?!" One escalates the emotions, and one calms the emotions.

Now you can begin to have a conversation about what can happen next instead of it all shutting down. Your goal is to eventually get into problem-solving mode, but you can't do that first. First, you have to say "yes." After that, you can start to have a different conversation.

The next time your partner is upset in any way, I want you to let them say their side of things. Try to *really* listen to what they're saying and identify how they're feeling. Then,

I want you to say "yes." I want you to empathize first with their feelings about what's going on. Let them know you understand what they're saying. **It doesn't mean you agree** with what they're saying, but you want them to know that you can understand that they feel a certain way, even if you don't understand why. From there, the door is open to many conversations and deepening your relationship.

REAL-LIFE EXAMPLE

Ben came to me because he was having trouble communicating and connecting to his wife, Mina. One of the biggest frustrations for Ben was Mina's "constant complaining" about her family.

"The other day she's telling me about a problem she's having with her sister," Ben began. "She got off the phone super upset that her sister isn't helping more with their mom, who's aging and living on her own. This sister expects Mina to do everything. Mina was going on and on about how her sister just dumps everything in her lap. I think Mina feels overwhelmed and guilty since we're so busy with our own family and it's super hard to find time for her mom. When I try to help, she jumps down *my* throat. I'm just trying to help! Why is she mad at me?!"

"Can I ask what you suggested to Mina?" I asked.

"Well, I've told her to try not speaking to her sister anymore or just not doing anything with their mom, which will force the sister to take some action."

"And how is your tone when you're offering these suggestions?" I asked.

Ben thought a bit and then replied, "Well, if I'm honest I guess I'm annoyed. She's been complaining and acting like a victim forever. I kind of want her to do something or just shut up about it at this point."

I told Ben that first, I didn't think his suggestions were really doable for Mina, which likely made her more frustrated and left her feeling misunderstood and not supported or "heard." I proceeded to teach Ben everything you just learned in this chapter. At the end of my little teach, I told him he needed to really start listening when Mina shared and match her emotion, but not tone. I told him to empathize (Say Yes First) and to focus on being patient in these conversations and not getting into "fix it" mode.

I didn't see Ben again for a little over a month due to some scheduling issues, but when he came back to the office, things had clearly shifted.

"I need to tell you, Abby, I thought this would never work," Ben began. "I felt like, as soon as I started giving in to Mina's complaints—that's how I saw this Say Yes First thing—that she'd go on and on and it would never end! But I gave it a try and, you know what? The opposite happened! It was like magic! I just really listened and tried to think about how I'd feel in this situation. I knew I'd mostly feel frustrated and maybe a little hopeless since nothing seemed to change. So, I said that to her. It was like a light went on in her head because she really looked at me differently. Next thing I know, we're totally talking about the issues with her sister and she asked me for some ideas—other than what I've mentioned before—to help her really problem-solve this and we came up with some great solutions that she can work with."

ACTION TIPS

Tip #1:

Remember that your amygdala can't turn on when you're using your prefrontal cortex. So you want to keep yourself in this other part of your brain as much as possible. For one week, start your day with a list of what you're grateful for, especially as it relates to your partner. Set an alarm for five minutes each morning and simply write as much as you can for five minutes.

Tip #2:

Send your partner a text each day with one thing you appreciate about them. Try to send a different appreciation every day for one week.

For you overachievers, if you like these Action Tips but want *more*, you can download my FREE Bonus Toolkit at *www.abbymedcalf.com/bonustoolkit*

CHAPTER EIGHT

KEY #6: ASK QUESTIONS AND DON'T SAC YOUR RELATIONSHIP

Tell me if this scene is familiar to you. You walk in the house and your partner is cooking dinner, watching TV or at their computer. You say, "Honey, I'm home!" They don't stop what they're doing or even look up, but yell out, "How was your day?" You yell back "good" or "fine" while you go change out of your work clothes or put away the groceries.

This scenario plays out millions of times a day in homes all across the country. The problem is that this interaction is a total missed opportunity! You've been apart for hours and this is a chance to reconnect! This is a chance to set the tone for the evening, but everyone is just lost in their own agenda and needs. This is your relationship on autopilot and it's time to consciously drive this car!

Questions like "How was your day?" or "What did you do today?" are the worst. These are bad, useless questions and are basically a dismissal. You're acknowledging the other person but letting them know you don't really have much

The 10 Keys to Being Happily Married

effort to put into a conversation with them. Let's face it, *you already know the answer you're going to get* to any of these questions: You ask, "How was your day?" and they answer "Fine" or "Good." Maybe you ask, "What did you do today?" and they answer "Nothing." Fine, good and nothing are throwaways. You might as well not have asked any question that gives you one of these words as the answer.

These questions suck because they're just polite space-fillers. They don't create connection, meaning, kindness, appreciation or love. They don't even give you basic information. Again, they're a waste of time.

So, what *should* you say or do when your partner gets home and you haven't seen one another all day? A few things. First, of all, get off your ass, stop what you're doing and go greet them at the door. Give them a hug or real kiss. Make eye contact and tell them something like, "I'm so happy you're home," or "I missed you today," or "Glad you're back… is there anything I can help you with?" All of these are awesome ways to connect. It literally only takes a few seconds, but makes a world of difference.

But greeting one another after a long day apart isn't the only missed opportunity for connection. It's the rest of the conversations all that evening that are also points of often-missed bonding. Our day-to-day exchanges with our partners are the place where the most frustrations, misunderstandings and resentments pop up. It's our general language and dialogue patterns that get us into trouble.

I have a key solution for this. I always say that your first job is to never **SAC** your relationship. This means, don't give **S**uggestions, offer **A**dvice or **C**riticize. When you offer suggestions or advice to your partner, it's almost never wanted. First of all, if your partner wants a suggestion or advice, they'll ask you. Think about it right now: when was the last time your partner asked you for a suggestion or your advice on something? Oh, can't remember? Exactly!

When you give unsolicited suggestions or advice, you're basically telling your partner that they're doing something wrong or that they can't figure something out for themselves. It's really a subtle form of blame or disapproval, which is about you, not your partner. Maybe you're frustrated that they keep complaining about their friend, Fran. Maybe you're impatient that they still don't get themselves ready quicker. Maybe you're resentful that they spend more money than you. I'm not saying you never have good intentions. Maybe you're worried that they're going to get in an accident because they keep looking at their phone while they drive.

The problem is that unsolicited suggestions are almost never taken well in the end. Even if your partner smiles and agrees in the moment, you'll likely notice that they don't follow through on your excellent advice. It's because, deep down, they're resentful and resistant to these ideas of yours.

Think about how you react when someone tells you what you "should" do. How does it feel? How do you feel when someone tells you a different way you could do something when you never asked for their opinion? You'll see that it's not a great feeling.

Criticizing your partner also needs to go away. There is NEVER a good outcome from this. It makes your partner feel like poop and generally makes them angry and resentful. It also pretty much NEVER changes their behavior. So, WTF? Why are you doing it?!

You might be thinking right now, "Well, what's left, Abby? If I can't give suggestions, offer advice or criticize, what's left? If my partner is doing something I don't like, what am I supposed to do, just suck it up?" That's a good question. And that's just what I want you to do. **Ask questions**. Instead of SACing your relationship, I want you to ask questions:

- "What do you think that means?"
- "How can I help you with this?"
- "What do you think your/our next steps should be?"
- "What did you think I meant by what I just said?"

My life is always better when I ask more questions and make less statements. Next time you're speaking with your partner, *try to ask questions only*. This is an amazing exercise to attempt anywhere in your life: at work, with your kids or your best friend. It's hard to do, but it will give you a whole new perspective on a situation. You will quickly realize that a lot of what you say to others all day is about getting your agenda passed, as opposed to really listening and communicating with those around you.

Questions are powerful. They make the brain think about a behavior, which actually increases the chances that the person (aka: your partner) will take an action. In fact, research[35] over the last 40 years has found that the more the brain thinks about a behavior, the more likely it is that the person will absorb and take part in that behavior.

Let me ask you a question right now: What did you have for dinner last night? Boom! I just hijacked your brain. When I asked you that question you, no doubt, started to think about what you had for dinner yesterday. I know it seems simple, but that little task has big implications because, by asking you that question, I momentarily commandeered your thought process and focused it completely on food.

---

35 https://www.ncbi.nlm.nih.gov/pmc/articles/PMC2440575/

Abby Medcalf

You didn't consciously tell your brain to think about dinner last night; it went there automatically because questions prompt a mental reflex known as "instinctive elaboration." In his book *The Science of Selling*, author David Hoffeld says that when a question is asked, it takes over the brain's thought process. And when your brain is reflecting about the answer to a question, it can't think about anything else.[36]

I'm about to hijack your brain again with another question. What does lemon juice taste like? Even though you only just thought about lemon juice for a few seconds, something completely beyond your control happened: you started to salivate. Right now, you're salivating and can almost taste how tart drinking lemon juice would be. You might even squint your eyes a little as you think about drinking some.

> What this shows is that just thinking about doing something can actually alter your body chemistry somewhat and shift your perceptions.

When you ask your partner a question, it puts them in a conscious state where *they want to find answers to that question you just posed*. It puts them into thinking and problem-solving mode, which is what you want. It means they're out of any fight-flight-freeze mode and into the rational and compassionate part of their brain (which you learned about in the last chapter).

---

36   https://www.amazon.com/Science-Selling-Strategies-Influence-Decisions/dp/0143129325

Asking good questions gets people out of autopilot and into really thinking and communicating.

Instead of asking your partner how his/her day was, ask questions like:

- "If I could say one thing right now that would make tonight great, what would it be?"
- "What was the best thing that happened today?"
- "What was your least favorite part of the day?"
- "What interesting thing happened today?"

Basically, you want to ask anything that will give you an answer *other than* "good," "nothing" or "fine." *Asking good questions (we psychologist types call these "open-ended questions") gets people out of autopilot and into really thinking and communicating.*

Asking useless questions means you're missing the opportunity to connect with your partner. Too many missed opportunities add up to relationships with two people living separate lives instead of as true partners.

REAL-LIFE EXAMPLE

Jake was fed up with his partner, Saanvi, by the time he came to see me. He lamented that they just couldn't seem to communicate, no matter what he'd tried in the past.

"I'm that guy who's read all the self-help books and gone to workshops. I've tried everything, and nothing works. We end up arguing over the stupidest things and it makes me crazy! It's clear to me that we've had years of building resentments, and we need therapy to dig into all that, but she refuses to go. I don't know if it's a cultural thing, because she's Indian, or what, but she says that we should just be able to work this out ourselves. I also don't know if she thinks it's as bad as I do."

It was clear that Jake had a story written in his mind about how he and Saanvi would need years of therapy to make a difference. I had a different idea: Go nuclear with the "love questions" bomb.

I told him that I wanted him to completely stop making statements to Saanvi for the next week, unless it was to answer a direct question about logistics (i.e., "What time will you be home for dinner?"). Anything else, I told him I wanted him to stop and ask a meaningful, thoughtful and/or loving question. Although he looked at me like I was crazy, he agreed.

Jake came back the next week very animated: "OK, you're totally onto something with this question thing! I don't understand exactly why it works, but I can't believe how much things have changed in just a week. At dinner last week, Saanvi started to complain about her commute (again). Previously, we've had lots of bad conversations about her commute. Basically, she hates it, but we can't afford to live near where she works right now, and I only have about a 20-min-

The 10 Keys to Being Happily Married

ute commute. We agreed when we bought our house that it was the best place to live, but now she's been commuting an hour and a half each way for almost three years and she's sick of it.

"First of all, it was really hard not to make my usual statements about this. You know, telling her that she agreed that this was the best course when we bought the house, and how we're saving so we can move within five years hopefully. This would always get her more upset, and then I would get angry and defensive and we just ended up having this circular argument that made me nuts because nothing ever changed!

"I stopped myself from making my usual comments and remembered what you said. I needed to ask loving questions. It was hard at first but got easier once we got talking. So, first I said, 'It's hard for me to hear that this commute is killing you. I love you, and I hate seeing you miserable. I'm sorry it sucks so bad. What else do you think we can do about this? What haven't we thought of as a solution?' At first, she said, 'Oh, nothing. I know I shouldn't complain. It's just how it has to be.'

"I've got to tell you, Abby, I was shocked that just me speaking in this way got her to calm down! Right away she admitted that she shouldn't complain and there was nothing to be done! I couldn't believe it. And the old me would have taken a victory lap and been done with the conversation. But, I really got to thinking about how I really am sad that she's so unhappy. When she first agreed to this commute, she had no way to know how bad it would be! Suddenly, I really wanted us to figure out a solution for her. So, I asked again. I said, 'No, I understand why you're complaining and I'm sorry I usually shut down this conversation, but I really think we should brainstorm some ideas for how to make this better. Let's make a list of just *anything* that could be an option, no matter how crazy we think it is.'

"We didn't get out a pen and paper or anything, but we actually started to brainstorm ideas. Some we've discussed before and had previously dismissed, but we brought them up again anyway. We talked about her taking the train, doing a casual carpool so she didn't have to always drive, renting a small place where she could stay overnight near work a couple of nights per week, so she didn't have to commute every day, looking for a new job, all kinds of things.

"What's crazy is that, even though we don't have any permanent solutions yet, we're getting along so much better. We're talking more and she's more open and less defensive. It's like we're suddenly on the same team, trying to find answers together. Instead of the commute being her problem, it's something we're trying to solve together, which is making us feel more connected, not just about this, but everywhere in our relationship."

ACTION TIPS

Tip #1:

Focus on asking questions all day tomorrow or sometime soon. I'm not saying you can never make a statement but, for 24 hours, try to ask as many good questions as you can. Notice how much you tend to lecture or nag your partner, yourself, your friends, coworkers, and kids. It's an amazing exercise if you give it a chance. Notice the change in your conversations when you ask questions instead of making statements. Don't forget to ask yourself questions even during that internal dialogue in your head all day. Instead of berating yourself for not getting to the gym, ask yourself "What's really stopping me from getting to the gym?"

Tip #2:

Start stepping up, leaning in and asking questions. *Here are some questions to ask yourself:*

- Are you checking in to see if your partner had a rough day?
- Are you actively doing things with the intention of service and a feeling of safety for your partner?
- Do you do nice things without being asked?
- Are you keeping your side of the street clean?
- Do you need reminders to take care of your life?
- Are you telling your partner sincerely and consistently how appreciative and grateful you are?
- Do you validate your partner's emotions?
- Are you answering your partner's bids most of the time?

- Do you contribute in a constructive way to planning, rides, meals and logistics?

For you overachievers, if you like these Action Tips but want *more*, you can download my FREE Bonus Toolkit at *www.abbymedcalf.com/bonustoolkit*

CHAPTER NINE

KEY #7: BRING YOUR SEXY BACK

You can't talk about the keys to happy and successful relationships without talking about sex and intimacy. The big problem when we start talking about sex and intimacy is that a lot of people think these words are synonymous and so confuse them…often! Here's the deal: you can have sex without intimacy and you can definitely have intimacy without sex, and this is at the core of many of the arguments and confusion couples experience. Men generally like to have sex to feel closer (feel intimate) and women generally have to feel close (feel intimate) to want sex. (I tell you, it's a damn miracle that any heterosexual couples ever make it work).

So what the heck is intimacy, anyway? Intimacy is simply the experience of emotional closeness. Intimacy includes feeling

- Connected
- Like you and your partner are a team
- Like your partner "gets" and understands you

The 10 Keys to Being Happily Married

- That your partner has your back

A lot of times, people are looking to feel intimacy or closeness, but confuse it with wanting sex. They then pursue sex, don't get the feeling they're looking for (and might even feel worse after having sex) and then continue to try to chase that close feeling they desire by having *more* sex. In the end, they're disappointed over and over again because, much like drugs or alcohol, sex without intimacy is a short-term solution with no long-term gains.

Now, I'm not saying you can ignore sex and still have a happy, intimate and fulfilled relationship, because you *generally* can't (unless you're over 80—although I have worked with people having sex in their 80s!). Sex is absolutely important! In fact, researchers have found that sex plays an even bigger role than money when it comes to couples reporting satisfaction and happiness in their relationship.[37]

However, the research does *not* show that having *more* sex equals being "more happy." If you want to know the actual "number," the research shows that having sex once a week is the sweet spot for couples staying happy and satisfied over the long haul.[38]

But sex is only part of a much larger equation when I'm talking about being truly close to your partner. In addition to sex, you also need an intimate connection with your partner to be happy. Researcher and social psychologist Amy Muise says, "It's important to maintain an intimate connection with your partner without putting too much pressure on engaging in sex as frequently as possible."[39]

---

37 http://spp.sagepub.com/content/early/2015/11/16/1948550615616462.abstract
38 http://spp.sagepub.com/content/early/2015/11/16/1948550615616462.abstract
39 http://psyc.info.yorku.ca/health-profiles/index.php?dept=&mid=1456353

So, where do you start? I break physical intimacy down into five main components: looking, touching, hugging, kissing and sex. They're all important, so let's break down each one.

Looking

Looking is all about how you interact with your partner without touch and with minimal or no words. Are you checking out your wife's ass when she walks away? Are you lusting after your partner's shoulders when he stretches? Do you appreciate how your partner took some extra time with their appearance today? Did you say how much you like your partner's eyes? Appreciating your partner's physical appearance in some way is what looking is all about. I love feeling my man's eyes on me when I walk into a room. He doesn't have to touch me or say a word, but I know he's thinking about me and that makes me feel close to him.

This isn't about having a perfect body or just being a sexual object (although that can be nice, too). It's about being the center of someone's attention and having priority when you're in their presence. If you get to a party first and your partner walks in later, don't just give them a perfunctory peck on the cheek and keep on talking to Jane from down the street. Instead, stop what you're doing and watch them walk toward you. Greet them with your eyes before they get to you. Let them know you're excited they've arrived and create a connection before continuing with what you're doing or saying.

Touching

The next part of physical intimacy is touching. How many times do you touch your partner every day? Recent studies have shown that we touch our cell phones over 2,000 times per day (!) and Apple recently confirmed that iPhone users unlock their phones 80 times every day, which breaks down to about six or seven times per hour![40] How many times an hour do you touch your partner? If that's too much to think about, how about how many times per day?

Touch is one of the most basic and necessary of all human needs. In fact, babies who are deprived of touch exhibit stunted growth and delayed cognitive and motor skills; are more likely to develop diabetes, heart disease and obesity; and suffer more mental illnesses, including everything from psychosis to depression.[41]

But touch isn't just important for babies; it works with grownups, too. In his book *Touch*, author David Linden discusses a 2010 study by the National Basketball Association: "Researchers found that teams that celebrated successful plays with hugs, high-fives, fist bumps and other kinds of touch early in the season subsequently displayed more cooperative, selfless behavior on the court and were more successful as the season progressed."[42]

The importance of touch is key for couples also. Linden calls interpersonal touch "a crucial form of social glue." He goes on to say, "It can bind partners into lasting couples… fostering emotions of gratitude, sympathy and trust."

Hugging

As we take touching to the next level, we get to hugging. In her book "The How of Happiness," renowned happiness re-

---

[40] *http://www.businessinsider.com/dscout-research-people-touch-cell-phones-2617-times-a-day-2016-7*
[41] http://www.washingtonpost.com/wp-dyn/content/article/2010/04/23/AR2010042302223.html?tid=a_inl
[42] https://www.amazon.com/Touch-Science-Hand-Heart-Mind/dp/0143128442

searcher and author Sonja Lyubormirsky states that hugging is good for you and makes you happier.[43]

What's the special sauce that makes hugs so magical? The secret ingredient in hugs (and many physical touches) is something called oxytocin. Oxytocin is both a neurotransmitter and a hormone that's released mostly in response to different forms of social contact, but it's really abundant in skin-to-skin contact.

Oxytocin is a major player as it provides health benefits, promotes bonding and makes us want to touch those we love *more*. But its most amazing feat is that it reduces the reactivity of your amygdala (that part of the brain I keep talking about that's in charge of fear, anxiety and aggression). Basically, it tells it to sit down and chill out, so hugging actually makes you calmer!

Kissing

The third super-important part of physical intimacy is kissing. In her book *The Science of Kissing*, author Sheril Kirshenbaum[44] tells us about a ten-year-long German study that found that men who kissed their wives before leaving for work lived, on average, five years longer, and earned 20 to 30 percent *more* than men who left the house without that goodbye smooch. If that's not enough, the study also showed that those men who *didn't* kiss their wives before leaving in the morning were 50 percent more likely to get into a car accident that day (the researchers didn't think kissing created a force field around you, but thought that the kissers were probably starting their day with a positive attitude, which leads to a healthier lifestyle).

---

43   https://www.amazon.com/How-Happiness-Approach-Getting-Life/dp/0143114956
44   *http://www.sherilkirshenbaum.com/books/*

The 10 Keys to Being Happily Married

In other research, the Touch Research Institute in Miami found that "the amount a couple kissed was proportional to their stated level of relationship satisfaction."[45]

Think about how often you kiss your partner. I've mentioned previously in this book that it's a great idea to greet your partner at the door when they come home and give them a kiss. Personally, my partner and I often have a little makeout session when we first see one another after a long day. It's totally fun and flirty, and puts me in an excellent mood to make dinner!

It's also a great idea to think of kissing your partner any time of day before you go your separate ways. It's about a connection before leaving one another. Also, think of the last time you had just a steamy makeout session with your partner. Has it been awhile? Often, the art of kissing gets lost in just having sex. Making time to just kiss for a few minutes and not have it lead to sex can be fun and change things up a bit.

Sex

Now that we've covered looking, touching, hugging and kissing, it's time to finally talk about sex! You've likely heard the popular statistic that men think about sex every seven seconds, or 8,000 times per day. The problem is that there is absolutely no research to back this claim! From the limited research that *has* been done, it seems that men think about sex one to two times per hour, but think about food and sleep just as much. Women think about sex a little less than men, statistically, but that's not really the point.[46]

The real issue with how often people think about sex isn't related to their gender, but to their degree of comfort with

---

45   *http://www6.miami.edu/touch-research/*
46   *https://www.psychologytoday.com/blog/the-sexual-continuum/201112/how-often-do-men-and-women-think-about-sex*

sexuality (also known as erotophilia). People who score higher on tests for erotophilia think about sex more than people who are uncomfortable with sexuality. So, the real question is how comfortable are you and your partner with talking about sex? A great sex life comes more from these conversations than almost anything else.

Marriage expert John Gottman has conducted studies that show that 70 percent of women don't have orgasms with sexual intercourse alone, so, to make sex appealing (and even create situations where women are the initiators), men need to think of sex being more than just touch the boobs, go for the goods.[47] *There needs to be more beforehand* most of the time. It doesn't need to be hours of foreplay, but there needs to be more of that connection, physical intimacy and thoughtfulness.

This is where porn becomes a problem. Now, I like porn as much as the next gal and it can have a fun place within a relationship. The problem is that, in porn movies, women are always wet, ready to go any time, and have orgasms every five seconds or so. As anyone reading this knows: that ain't real life. It sets real women up to look frigid or "hard to please" when, in fact, that's not true.

Despite common folklore, the research shows that women say "yes" to sex 75 percent of the time![48] A lot of the issues arise *after* she's said "yes" and you've gone into the bedroom (or shower, or closet or tabletop for you lucky few). The problem often centers around foreplay. That's because a lot of men think that foreplay is the stuff you do to turn on a woman right before you have sex. These men are only partly right.

---

47   https://www.gottman.com/blog/what-do-women-really-want/
48   http://www.esquire.com/entertainment/a7290/survey-of-american-women-0510/

The 10 Keys to Being Happily Married

For women, foreplay isn't just about the minutes before intercourse. Foreplay for women happens all day long when their man is warm, tender, thoughtful and kind. Show me a woman who feels appreciated in her relationship and you'll see someone who looks a lot more like those women in porn: turned on without their man necessarily having to do a whole lot in the bedroom (although that's nice, too).

In a large-scale survey of people in 24 countries, researchers found that couples who report a "great sex life" do the following:[49]

- Have makeout sessions and kiss each other passionately (another German study found that men who kiss their wives every day live five years longer than the men who didn't)
- Kiss and touch non-erotically every day
- Cuddle together non-sexually
- Say "I love you" and mean it every day.

At the end of the day, sex is something you only do with your partner and no one else.* This is the one thing you share as a couple that you don't share with anyone else. But you need to remember that intimacy is a skill that takes practice. I don't believe everyone just wants more sex—I think what people really crave is more intimacy.

*(I want to give a shout out to any polyamorous couples reading this or to anyone who agrees to have additional sexual partners within or without the "marriage bed," but I'm speaking here to the "general" population of monogamous couples).

---

[49] http://www.who.int/reproductivehealth/publications/general/lancet_2.pdf

REAL-LIFE EXAMPLE

When Tara came to me, she was worried that her husband, Lucas, was going to leave her: "We've been married 14 years and have two children, ages 7 and 10. We both work and between that and taking care of the kids, sex has taken a huge nosedive over the years. Lucas always wants more sex, but I just don't want any part of it. I'm too tired. I'm just afraid he's going to get it somewhere else or leave me because of it. It makes him mad that I say no as much as I do."

As you might imagine, this is a VERY common scenario that I see with couples all too often. They think

- It's OK that the heat leaves the relationship and expect this to happen. They expect a steady decline.
- They're just too tired to think about sex or being sexy with all the demands of work and life (believe it or not, this also happens to couples who don't have kids).

The issue is that couples try to jump into "having more sex," but there's no foreplay. I'm not talking about the foreplay right before actually having sex. I'm talking about the foreplay that happens all day.

So I told Tara to start focusing on foreplay all day. This wasn't about waiting for Lucas to do the right things to "get her in the mood." This was about Tara doing the right things to get herself in the mood!

"You can't control what Lucas is doing, but you *can* control your own thoughts and actions," I told her. "Start with the morning. I want you to put on matching lingerie under your clothing. When you get dressed, think of wearing things that make you feel pretty, if not sexy. Send Lucas a sext during the day or maybe even a provocative picture of yourself. Think about sex during the workday a little.

The 10 Keys to Being Happily Married

Maybe even take a minute to touch yourself during the day and masturbate a little, but don't have an orgasm. When Lucas comes home from work, give him a "real" kiss when he walks in the door. Stop and make out a little. Then, see how you feel."

Tara gave me a *very* skeptical look and said she'd try but couldn't see herself sneaking off to the bathroom at work and masturbating. I told her to see what she could push herself to do.

When I saw Tara again she almost giggled as she told me, "I can't believe that worked! I did what you said last Wednesday. I wore cute undies under my clothes and I sent Lucas a picture of me in them. That blew him away! I did play with myself for just a minute when I went to the bathroom at work and I felt very naughty! It was funny how being "bad" made me feel sexy. Putting myself in that sexy frame of mind all day did make me want sex later! I was shocked. I'm the one who jumped Lucas that night. We've had sex two more times this week. I feel kind of powerful!"

I let Tara know that this wasn't necessarily how I wanted her to be for the rest of her life, but I wanted her to see that she's in charge of her sexuality and her sex life. Like many wives, she was waiting on Lucas to do certain things to get her in the mood. That's all well and good, but getting *herself* in the mood was empowering.

Over time, she started to share with Lucas more and more about what she needed and wanted from him so she'd feel more attracted to him and he was more open to listening *and delivering now that he could see that more sex was possible.*

As we met over time, Tara said their sex life would go up and down, but what she noticed most of all was that putting her attention on sex helped move the energy forward instead of it staying stagnant and feeling negative.

If you want to lose weight, you've got to focus on your food *over the course of the* day, not just at one meal. If you want to save money, you have to focus on your spending *over the course of the* day, not just during one transaction. If you want to rev up the physical intimacy in your relationship, you need to focus on it over the course of the day, not just when you're having sex.

ACTION TIPS

Tip #1:

Shut the door! All that goes on with sharing a home and life leads to a lot of overfamiliarity. This overfamiliarity makes it hard to keep physical intimacy fresh and fun. I want you to make sure to keep some things private. Need to pee? Close the damn bathroom door! Need to fart? Leave the room. Have some weird skin tag on your inner thigh? Show it to your best friend or your doctor, not your partner. Think you smell a little ripe, but you just want to drop into bed? Get your ass up and take a quick shower first.

Tip #2:

When your partner walks in the house, stop whatever you're doing and physically go greet them at the door. Give them a kiss or hug (or both) and welcome them home. Make eye contact and be intentional with having them feel the love and happiness you feel that they're home.

Tip #3:

At times when you're together, focus on touching your partner often. Maybe every time you touch your phone, make sure you also touch your partner.

For you overachievers, if you like these Action Tips but want *more*, you can download my FREE Bonus Toolkit at *www.abbymedcalf.com/bonustoolkit*

CHAPTER TEN

KEY #8: BE POSITIVE

In 1986, the New York Mets were in the World Series with the Boston Red Sox. The Mets won the series in Game Seven, after battling back from a pretty much hopeless deficit in Game Six (being a diehard Mets fan, this was a huge day for me, but I digress).

In Game Six, New York Met Mookie Wilson hit an easy ground ball toward Red Sox first baseman, Bill Buckner, in the bottom of the tenth inning. The ball very famously went through Buckner's legs and this mistake became the defining moment of his career. Now, the lead had already been blown (the Red Sox were ahead 3-0 in the sixth inning), but Bill Buckner became the scapegoat for that series and pictures of the ball going through Bill Buckner's legs follow him (I'm sure until this day).[50]

What's really amazing though is that *Bill Buckner was a great player.* He had an incredible twenty-year career in baseball. He accumulated over 2,700 hits (174 of these were home runs), won a batting title in 1980, had a career batting average of .289, and had 1208 RBI's. I'll say it again. Bill Buck-

---

50   *http://www.baseball-almanac.com/ws/yr1986ws.shtml* and https://en.wikipedia.org/wiki/1986_World_Series

The 10 Keys to Being Happily Married

ner was a *great* ball player. However, fans (and I'm sure Bill) will always remember that error in Game Six.[51]

We've all had Game Six moments. And we all remember them, with often cringe-worthy shudders and shakes of our head. Why is it so easy to recall the bad, but so difficult to enjoy the good?

Renowned social psychologist Roy Baumeister has found in his research that "Bad emotions, bad parents and bad feedback have more impact than good ones. Bad impressions and bad stereotypes are quicker to form and more resistant to disconfirmation than good ones." This is why you're more upset if you lose $20 than happy if you find $20. This is why you can give a dinner party where everyone raves about the food, except the broccoli was a little overcooked so you focus on the broccoli. To bring even more fun to the negativity party, *bad events wear off more slowly than good ones,* which keeps them in our conscious mind even longer![52]

Clifford Nass, of Stanford University, explains that there are physiological as well as psychological reasons why we all have the general tendency to remember the bad and not the good: "The brain handles positive and negative information in different hemispheres...Negative emotions generally involve more thinking, and the information is processed more thoroughly than positive ones. Thus, we tend to ruminate

---

51 *http://www.baseball-reference.com/players/b/bucknbi01.shtml*

52 https://www.google.com/url?sa=t&rct=j&q=&esrc=s&source=web&cd=1&ved=0ahUKEwijwozamIDPAhVQx2MKHVDtB44QFggcMAA&url=https%3A%2F%2Fcarlsonschool.umn.edu%2Ffile%2F49901%2Fdownload%3Ftoken%3DGoY7afXa&usg=AFQjCNGNSuNE_lrzds7Wbsb6guWhz0B-Vyg&bvm=bv.131783435,d.cGc

more about unpleasant events—and use stronger words to describe them—than happy ones."[53]

So, how does all this apply to your relationship? Well, we now know that **one negative interaction does more *harm* in your marriage than one positive interaction *helps* your marriage.**[54]

Not only that, but, based on the work of John Gottman and his marriage research laboratory at the University of Washington, we know that the magic ratio you need to have a happy relationship is 5:1. In other words,

> *you need to have five times as many positive interactions with your partner as negative ones for your relationship to be stable.*

What?!?! That's right. For every five wonderful, awesome things your partner does, they only have to screw up *once* for you to say, "I knew she'd start nagging me again!" or "I knew he wouldn't be able to keep this up!"

Dr. Gottman is actually able to *predict* divorce based on this ratio. He's found that unhappy couples tend to have

---

[53] https://www.amazon.com/Man-Who-Lied-His-Laptop-ebook/dp/1617230014/ref=sr_1_1?s=-books&ie=UTF8&qid=1473356936&sr=1-1&keywords=The+Man+Who+Lied+to+His+Laptop%3A+What+Machines+Teach+Us+About+Human+Relationships"

[54] http://www.nytimes.com/2012/03/24/your-money/why-people-remember-negative-events-more-than-positive-ones.html?pagewanted=all&_r=1

The 10 Keys to Being Happily Married

more negative than positive interactions.[55] This is *not* to say that you can't have arguments or disagreements with your partner. In fact, these disagreements are necessary. But, as Gottman says, "Happy couples deliver positive emotional messages, even when they don't see eye to eye."

So, how do you deal with this 5:1 ratio? How do you level the playing field so your mind doesn't skew your relationship in such a negative and unrealistic way? One of the easiest and most effective tools is to turn neutral events into positive ones. It's something former Google employee #107 and current happiness author Chade-Meng Tan calls recognizing "thin slices of joy."

He explains it this way: "Right now, I'm a little thirsty, so I will drink a bit of water. And when I do that, I experience a thin slice of joy both in space and time. It's not like 'Yay!' It's like, 'Oh, it's kind of nice.'"

We experience this type of thing all the time, but usually these experiences are unremarkable: eating something when you're hungry, not being in pain, the sensation of stepping from a hot street into an air-conditioned restaurant, the moment of connection when you hug your kid or pet your dog. Although they only last two or three seconds, these small moments add up. According to Tan, the more you notice these little moments of joy, the more you'll experience joy in your life as a whole.[56]

"Thin slices of joy occur in life everywhere… and once you start noticing it, something happens, you find it's always

---

[55] *https://www.gottman.com/blog/the-positive-perspective-dr-gottmans-magic-ratio/*
[56] https://www.amazon.com/Joy-Demand-Discovering-Happiness-Within-ebook/dp/B0166JFH3I/ref=sr_1_2?ie=UTF8&qid=1535476947&sr=8-2&keywords=chademeng+tan&dpID=418jBkEFDgL&preST=_SY445_QL70_&dpSrc=srch

there. Joy becomes something you can count on," says Tan. The bottom line: you're familiarizing your mind with joy, so you start to see it more and more often. If you remember the reticular activating system (RAS) you read about earlier in this book, you'll see why this is true from a "brain science" point of view. In this case, you're telling your RAS to look for good things, and it'll obey and start showing you the things you were previously missing that fall into this "good" category.

Think about your relationship and how you can identify "thin slices of joy": The feeling you get when you warm up your cold feet on your partner in bed at night (or is that just me?); appreciating a home-cooked meal; gratitude that your partner always makes sure there's toilet paper in the house; the relief you feel when you go to pay a bill and there's money in the bank because your partner works and contributes. All of these are likely things you don't think much about, at least not consistently. Yet, they are all things that could (and should) go in the positive or "win" column.

If your partner screws something up (which they will), but you've been counting all these things as positives instead of ignoring them as neutrals, that 5:1 ratio won't be so lopsided.

> The good news is that being unhappy is just a habit and habits can be changed.

Your brain is always looking for the easier way of doing things so it can conserve energy. This effort toward efficiency results in what we call "habits." Research shows that as many as 40 percent of our daily actions are based on habits, not conscious decisions.

In his book *The Power of Habit*, author Charles Duhigg describes habits as a three-part loop:[57]

- **An External Cue/Trigger**: something that happens in your environment (e.g., you walk into the house after work)

- **The Routine**: this is what you usually do when this particular cue presents itself (e.g., go to the kitchen and rummage for something good to eat), and

- **The Reward**: a feeling of success (e.g., that "I'm home and life is going to be OK" feeling you get when you have yourself a snack at the end of a long day)

Habits are very resilient because learning and maintaining habits is stored in a part of the brain called the basal ganglia. The basal ganglia also plays a crucial role in the development of emotions and memory. Meanwhile, your decisions are made in a different part of the brain called the prefrontal cortex, which we've discussed earlier in this book. But as soon as a behavior becomes automatic, the decision-making part of your brain doesn't work.

When you're in the same fight over and over with your partner, it's a bad habit. You're on autopilot and don't realize it. The prefrontal cortex, or thinking part of your brain, is shut off so you can't remember the great tools you learned in this book.

Now, imagine having positive habit loops installed in your brain instead. Imagine that it was a habit to always look for the good your partner was doing or how caring they were.

---

[57] https://www.amazon.com/Power-Habit-What-Life-Business-ebook/dp/B0055PGUYU/ref=sr_1_4?s=digital-text&ie=UTF8&qid=1535477005&sr=1-4&keywords=power+of+habit&dpID=51Q4AwpPDkL&preST=_SY445_QL70_&dpSrc=srch

What if it was a habit to see the good, instead of the negative? Imagine the ass-kicking that 5:1 ratio would be getting!

REAL-LIFE EXAMPLE

Kate was completely fed up with her husband, Jonathan, when we met. Her exact words when I asked her to describe him: "He's lazy, unappreciative and defensive." Ouch.

I asked Kate for an example of Jonathan's behavior that supported her description. "Oh, I've got a million of them," she said, "But I'll give you the most recent. I asked him to clean the kitchen the other night after dinner because I didn't feel well. When I got up in the morning there was still jelly smeared on the counter from the day before, the pots in the dish drainer still had food stuck to them and he didn't come ask me if I felt better in the morning. He just took off for work assuming I'd handle the kids, dogs and everything like I always do."

When I asked more questions, it became clear that Jonathan was actually OK with helping out around the house (he worked full time and Kate was a stay-at-home mom) but would get "defensive" when Kate pointed out how he did things "wrong" (which he always did, according to Kate). "How can you clean the bathroom and not empty out the garbage can when it's overflowing? It's infuriating! If you're going to help, you should put in your best effort and really help!"

I explained to Kate that Jonathan was actually helpful, just not to her specifications, which didn't make him wrong or lazy. This constantly picking on what was wrong with what he did, instead of appreciating that he *did* help, was setting up a terrible habit. Of course Jonathan was defensive. He felt like he was doing all he could, and it was never good enough.

I said, "Can we look at the other morning another way? I know Jonathan didn't do a perfect job but, wouldn't you have had a lot more work to do if he hadn't at least tried to clean? It sounds like he got the kitchen pretty much all clean, everything in the dishwasher, floor swept, and what he couldn't fit in the dishwasher he at least tried to clean by hand. I know it wasn't a perfect job, but what percentage of cleaning the kitchen do you think he actually did? I mean, how long did it take you to wipe the counter and clean those two pots a little better?"

She begrudgingly replied, "I guess he did about 90 percent of the work overall."

"If you got a 90 percent on a paper when you were in school, what grade would you get?" I asked.

"Well, that's an A-," she replied.

"So, you'd give him an A-, but you're sitting here going on and on about what a bad job he did. You're calling him lazy and unappreciative. Didn't he work all day, come home, deal with the kids and put them to bed and clean up the kitchen? I know he didn't do a perfect job, but what's the expectation? What are you focused on here?"

As we talked more, she admitted that Jonathan had told her he was tired of trying to help because it was never good enough. I then asked her to look for these thin slices of joy. I asked her to start to look for neutral things Jonathan did and to start appreciating them.

Within a couple of weeks, she was back in the office saying, "I started looking for Jonathan's 'good deeds,' as I started calling them, and realized they were everywhere. There was so much I wasn't counting because there was some part I didn't like. So, he'd take out the garbage but he wouldn't wipe out that can, so I didn't appreciate what he was doing. He always compliments me and thanks me for dinner or making him breakfast. He thanks me for picking up his dry cleaning. He's also really funny and makes me laugh. Once

I started focusing on all this, I felt kind of silly focusing on the small amount he wasn't doing 'right.'"

Kate's relationship with Jonathan began to quickly and drastically improve. As she started noticing the thin slices of joy, she became happier and more appreciative in her life. Her mood became contagious in her home and Jonathan and her kids started reacting positively to it.

Within a couple of months, Kate said, "Jonathan is actually doing more around the house. He's paying more attention and doing more without me even asking. It's amazing!"

I told her that there were likely two things happening here. First, he might not be doing more but, because she was noticing the thin slices of joy, she was noticing more of what he was already doing that she'd been missing before. Second, he *might* be doing more, but it was because he was feeling this acceptance and love from her, so he was likely more motivated to do things for her. In the end, it was probably some combination of the two. Either way, everyone was much happier, with minimal effort.

ACTION TIPS

Tip #1:

Look for Thin Slices of Joy: Be in the here and now in your day-to-day life and purposefully notice the joyful moments in your day, however short or small they may be. Notice how good it feels to stand in the shower with the warm water running down your body. Be aware of how the first thing you drink every day feels going down your throat and quenches your thirst (or need for coffee). Be in the moment when you kiss your partner or children goodbye as you leave for work. Take in the moment of happiness when a friend texts you or your partner says, "I love you."

This exercise contains the three components needed to build a successful habit:

- **The External Cue/Trigger**: the pleasant moment
- **The Routine**: noticing the moment, and
- **The Reward**: the feeling of joy itself

Take a few moments to "thin slice" two times per day, for the next week.

Tip #2:

In general, get your head around how you think and respond to your partner. For example, instead of asking "What's wrong?" ask, "What's right?" Instead of asking "Why me?" ask "What am I learning in this situation?" Instead of asking "What's broken and how do I fix it?" ask, "What's working and how can I do more of it?" Think about how you can build on a previous success and go from there.

For you overachievers, if you like these Action Tips but want *more*, you can download my FREE Bonus Toolkit at *www.abbymedcalf.com/bonustoolkit*

CHAPTER ELEVEN

KEY #9: KEEPING SCORE IN YOUR RELATIONSHIP MAKES YOU LOSE

There's a lot going on in today's marriages: commutes, work, deadlines, keeping the house together, fitting in time with friends, self-care and just the general maintenance of life leave many couples feeling exhausted at the end of the day. When you throw kids, pets or taking care of aging parents into that mix, it can tip couples right over the edge of time management.

With all of these things competing for your time and attention, people often end up looking to their partner to save the day, help out and "pull their weight." You start watching everything *they* do and comparing it to what *you* do. In effect, you start keeping score in your relationship. This inevitably leads to feelings of resentment, anxiety, frustration and disappointment. Not the feelings you want if you're looking for a connected, happy and satisfying relationship. Whether you've been together 10 months or 10 years, keeping score and competing often become an unwelcome component of many relationships.

How do you stop it? Well, first you have to realize what you're doing and why. **There are basically four ways that keeping score in your relationship is setting you up to lose:**

#1: Keeping Score Sets You Up on Opposite Sides

We say things like: "I drove Matt to baseball on Tuesday, so it's your turn to take Sophie to soccer practice on Thursday." Or, the one I hate the most: "It's your *turn* to put away the dishes."

Do you hear yourself? It's your *turn*?! Taking turns happens in games and sports. If you're treating your relationship like a game, I can tell you right now—you're going to lose! You want to know why? Because keeping score like this in your relationship puts you and your partner on *opposite teams*! Think about it: this sets one of you up to win, and one of you to lose. How do you expect to have a connected, loving relationship when there's an underlying tension of someone losing? This kind of thinking worms itself into the foundation of your relationship and, before long, you're going to see a lot of cracks, if not actual walls crumbling down.

I need you to get out of the keeping score mindset and instead think of you and your partner as being on the *same team*. This means you are **one shared resource**. So, pulling energy from your partner really means pulling energy from yourself. Your team becomes drained and it's hard to win the game when everyone is tapped out.

What do you do to stop this behavior? My answer is to *add* resources instead of always looking to your partner to fill in the blanks or "pick up the slack." Instead of thinking that it's your partner's turn to clean the bathroom, why not figure out how to hire a cleaning person so neither of you has to do it and you can use the resources of the couple for other, more important things (like having rock star sex, relaxing or finally getting to that dentist appointment you've been putting off?).

If you don't have money, you can do things like bartering (Hey best friend, can you help me clean the garage and I'll help you with X, buy you lunch or just give you my undying loyalty?) or you could try swapping (Hey mother of my kid's best friend that I barely speak to, can you carpool on Tuesdays and I'll do Thursdays?). There are *many* ways to add resources to your relationship instead of exhausting the players on your team. If you're both stressed and overwhelmed, it's not helping anyone.

> Remember that when you constantly look to your partner to "do their part," you're actually taking away from yourself.

#2: Keeping Score Stops You from Listening and Connecting

To explain how keeping score stops you from listening and connecting, I'm going to start with a Real-Life Example of a woman I was working with named Jamilla. Tell me if this sounds familiar.

It was Friday and Jamilla was doing her usual. She had set up carpools for the kids for the following week, shopped for and made dinner (and this was difficult because of little Nino's recently diagnosed gluten allergy), she'd emailed back and forth all day about some things she needed to do for a PTA meeting next Wednesday, she stopped and picked up her husband Don's new fishing reel *and* she scheduled a

The 10 Keys to Being Happily Married

guy to take down the big tree whose roots had made their driveway look like a skatepark. Don got home a little early from a business trip that day and thought it was a great idea to sneak in some sex before they had to go pick up the kids from their respective sports practices.

Jamilla was exhausted already and still had a full night of kids, homework, baths and more emails ahead of her. She'd time managed herself down to the second to get all this done. She did NOT factor in sex with Don. When she rebuffed his advances, he complained, "You never want to have sex anymore—you don't make time for me!" Jamilla was totally pissed at his response (they had "just" had sex on Sunday before he left for his business trip, after all). In her defense of herself, she quickly started to tick off her LONG list of all the things she'd done all week while he was gone as well as that day.

This is keeping score. You've got your scorecard (and it's full) so you think you're covered. Well, you're not and, once again, this competition puts you in the loser's seat.

As we discovered in session together, if it had been up to Don, he'd rather that Jamilla had ordered a pizza, the kids went to bed slightly stinky and he got in a quickie!

Jamilla's list meant nothing to him. The things on her list were all about what *she* deemed important and necessary, not Don. Essentially, he was right when he said that Jamilla didn't prioritize and make time for him.

Once Jamilla realized all of this through the work she was doing in our sessions (and at home with Don), she realized that she needed to stop thinking of herself as being on the opposing team.

"I was always comparing what he did, versus what I did. First of all, you can't really compare since we do such different things and both our contributions are important," she said. "But, mostly, I didn't realize how much I was always in competition with him until now. I was always storing things up on my scorecard to show that I was doing more so it was OK to demand certain things from him and so that it was OK to say no to sex and time together. What the heck have I been thinking?!

"Now, I make Don a priority and, since I've started doing that, he's been helping out more. He's more patient and understanding. I was so worried that he was going to take advantage of me, but the opposite has happened. He's got my back way more now. This idea of thinking of us as one shared resource has completely changed my mindset. When I take from him, I take from me. When he's happy and fulfilled, that replenishes our couples' pool, which helps me in the end!"

What's true for Jamilla and Don is true for you. If a strong marriage is your goal, and your partner tells you they feel ignored in some way, then listing all the ways you *don't* ignore them isn't the answer! Your scorecard doesn't matter to your partner!

Instead, ask your partner what they *would* like to see more of in the relationship. What could you do to let them know you're a priority? Reading off your list is about you being "right"—it's not about your partner (or you) being happy.

The next time you're in an argument with your partner and they ask for something, instead of listing all the things you *did* do (so how could they possibly feel that way?), listen to what they're saying and do that! Understand that, despite how much you've done, it's not what *your partner* wanted from you.

#3: Equal Time Doesn't Mean Equal Value

The third way that keeping score in your relationship makes you lose is because nothing in a relationship is "fair" or equal if you look at it from a time perspective. The problem with looking at your relationship from a time perspective is that it doesn't take into account the *value* of what's being done, irrespective of time.

I call this the lions and hyenas effect. You know how in a pride of lions, the females do the majority of the work? The lionesses hunt and care for the young, which takes up a majority of their waking hours. Meanwhile, the males are sleeping and lying around or looking for a willing female to have sex (this might remind you of another species). Seems unfair, no? Well, it's really not.

You see, those male lions have a few, very important jobs which are vital to the survival of the pride, but they just don't take as much time as the jobs the lionesses have. The males are all about defending and fighting when those hyenas come around. This is a big job and it's no less crucial than what the females do. *The fact that they don't have to defend as much as the females have to hunt is inconsequential.*

Think of your own home. You and your partner both do things for the family, but it likely takes up very different amounts of time or energy. Regardless of the time you put in, both of your "jobs" are valuable.

Another point close to this is that equal time doesn't mean equal bandwidth. Let me tell you about a woman I worked with named Beth. She and her husband both worked full time, but Beth actually had a longer commute so really was away more hours for work than her husband.

She came to me complaining about how her hubby wasn't pulling his weight. The grocery shopping was a real sticking point for her. When I asked enough questions, though, it became clear that it took her a lot less time to grocery shop than her husband. She was better at it and didn't hate it as much. I told her to do the grocery shopping even though she had less time in her workweek than he did.

For Beth, it took very little of her bandwidth or her mental energy to get the grocery shopping done. For her husband to do it took a huge amount of energy (searching for things in the supermarket, trying to remember what kind of milk they liked, etc.). I reminded her that, if they were a shared resource (she and her husband), then she'd be using up less resources in the relationship if she did the grocery shopping despite the fact that this means she put in more hours in the "work" of their relationship.

At the end of the day, Beth admitted that her husband did make her feel safe and loved and this was really the most important thing she needed. She was also grateful that while she was grocery shopping, he could be home taking care of the kids or even relaxing a bit so he was more fresh and had more energy by the time she got home and needed a break. Keeping score with how many hours they both put into things was a waste of time and was hurting the relationship while not honoring her partner's *very* valuable contributions.

#4: Being Happy for Your Partner Equals a Happy Marriage

The fourth and final way that keeping score in your relationship makes you lose is that when you keep score, you set yourself up to be competing with your partner. By default, this means you *won't* be happy when your partner shares good news. How can you be? If you're competing and they do well, it means you're losing! So, instead of being happy that your partner got a promotion, you end up thinking (or saying), "Well, good for you that you got a promotion and now get to travel to Europe for work. I'll just be stuck at home taking care of the kids!" When they get something good, you get resentful. You act as if they scored a goal and you're the loser watching it happen. Sound familiar?

The 10 Keys to Being Happily Married

Famed marriage expert John Gottman has shown in his research[58] that not being able to connect over each other's good news spells failure for many relationships. He calls these "disaster couples" and with these disaster couples he found that "when one person in the relationship shared the good news of, say, a promotion at work with excitement, the other would respond with wooden disinterest by checking his watch or shutting the conversation down with a comment like, 'That's nice.'"

Don't be a disaster couple! Remember, you're a shared resource. Stop focusing so much on yourself and focus on the two of you together. If one player on a basketball team is the greatest player ever, but never passes the ball and doesn't work with his teammates, they're never going to be champions. It's the *team* that makes it to the Finals, Super Bowl, Stanley Cup or World Series, not the individual. The only time one person wins something is in golf or tennis, and those are solo sports. Again, if you want the marriage to win, you need to stop keeping score for yourself. Be a team player and know that everyone on the team is valuable, not just the ones with the most playing time or scores.

Being there for your partner when the going gets rough is obviously important, but the research has shown that being there for your partner when the going goes *right* is actually more important for relationship satisfaction and happiness. So, make sure that you are your partner's biggest support and cheerleader. Be aware when your partner shares good news and show active interest in what they're telling you; be their biggest encouragement and source of excitement.

Get out of the "I win, you lose" attitude. Remember that although **disagreement is inevitable, conflict is optional**. This is a choice you need to make every time an issue arises.

---

[58] https://www.theatlantic.com/health/archive/2014/06/happily-ever-after/372573/

Abby Medcalf

No matter what else you do, stop keeping score and start seeing you and your partner as one shared resource!

The 10 Keys to Being Happily Married

ACTION TIPS

Tip #1:

Identify three resources you're going to *add* to the relationship instead of asking your partner to do it.

Tip #2:

If your partner complains about something (e.g., that you don't pay enough attention to them), make sure your immediate response is a question. Find out what you can do to make them feel more cared for. Ask them what they would like to see more of. Do NOT list all the things you've done for them or tell them why they shouldn't feel that way.

For you overachievers, if you like these Action Tips but want *more*, you can download my FREE Bonus Toolkit at *www.abbymedcalf.com/bonustoolkit*

CHAPTER TWELVE

KEY 10: FORGIVENESS

Welcome to the final chapter of *The 10 Keys to Being Happily Married, Even if Your Partner Won't Do a Thing*. From chapter to chapter, you've learned tools and strategies to take full responsibility and work on your relationship despite whatever your partner is (or isn't) doing.

This last chapter is truly all about you because now we're going to talk about forgiveness. You're going to learn what it is, what's it's not, why you care and the five-step process for shifting from any lingering resentments to peace and openness.

You might be thinking this chapter isn't for you. You might be thinking that you don't *have* anything to forgive or you might be thinking that you're the one that needs to be forgiven because you did something that feels, well, unforgiveable. I'm here to tell you that I've yet to meet a couple where neither partner had anything to forgive. If you're feeling any unhappiness, resentment, frustration, helplessness or hopelessness in your relationship, then forgiveness is certainly something that will help.

So, what is there to forgive? In *any* relationship, there are hurts that can build up. Even really good relationships have "stuff" that lingers. Maybe you don't feel appreciated. You cook dinner, work hard at your job all day or any number of things that your partner doesn't say "thank you" for.

Maybe you feel like your partner has been insensitive and they've hurt your feelings or made you angry because of something they've done or said. Maybe you feel wronged by your partner and that they "should have known better." You might have even made the dreaded statement, "If he loved me he would have done X," or "If she loved me she never would have done Y."

Maybe your partner forgot something important like your anniversary, birthday or that you told them you were getting a promotion today. There are many situations that can lead to you feeling disappointed, frustrated, enraged or hurt.

What do you usually do when you have something that keeps coming up in your relationship? What do you do when that thing your partner did just stays in your mind and you find yourself playing it like a bad movie over and over again? Or maybe it was one big thing (like infidelity, a really big lie or stealing) and you feel you just can't "forgive and forget?"

There are three main approaches you likely have when you're angry with your partner.

First: Direct Talk

Maybe you talked to your partner about what's bothering you, but it didn't resolve the issue, made you angrier or is just so "big" that it's taking multiple conversations. The bottom line here is that speaking directly to your partner isn't changing your feelings for the better. So direct talk didn't work.

Second: Sharing Squared

Another strategy you might have used in the past when you were upset with your partner was to call your best friend, speak to coworkers or basically pin down anyone who would listen and told them about the situation with your partner. You repeated the story over and over and over again. But talking about something over and over just gets *you* more upset. You start re-living whatever bad thing happened or was said and you just end up more sad or angry. To make matters worse, you got 10 different opinions about what you "should" do and that made you even more despondent. Reviewing old hurts, in our traditional ways, often doesn't help in the long-term.

We've all been there with a therapist or friend asking, "When did the abuse start?" or "How did it make you feel when your husband cheated on you?" As I've said before, you'll find that the more you speak about something terrible, the worse it often makes you feel. So, "sharing squared" didn't work.

Third: Brushing it Under the Rug

Lastly, maybe you tried brushing it under the rug. You just tried to "forgive and forget." The problem is that you can't muscle your way to forgiveness. The feelings don't magically go away because you *said* that you were going to forgive. The bad thing isn't forgotten and the thoughts just keep sneaking into your head. Naturally, you then push those feelings underground and they come out in unhealthy ways (rage, overeating, physical pain, alcohol or drug use, increased blood pressure, etc.). Brushing it under the rug didn't work.

So why *don't* these things work? These approaches don't work because when you're doing any of them, what essentially happens is that you create (more) resentment.

The 10 Keys to Being Happily Married

Resentment breaks down as "re," which means again, and "sense," which means to feel. So, re-sentment is really feeling something *again*. This situation is reminding you of something that's happened earlier in your relationship that bugged you before and now it's bugging you again, but it's compounded. You find yourself saying things like, "He *always* does this to me" or "She *never* X."

As soon as you hear yourself using these kinds of generalized words, I want you to stop and notice (you'll catch yourself because, at this point, you're an attention training ninja)! "Always" and "never" are not true words. Saying, "He or she never listens to me" doesn't work because there has certainly been at least one time that he or she did (maybe that was on your first date, but then you've got to ask yourself why you kept dating someone who only listened once, but I digress). It also doesn't work because your partner hears this and immediately dismisses it because they feel like they *have* listened, so now they really aren't listening to what you say because they think there's no winning with you. Even though they have "listened," they get no credit, so why bother? It's a nasty cycle.

The question to ask yourself when you're feeling resentful is, "What does this remind me of?" It must remind you of something, because that's the "always" or "never" feeling.

I recently met with a couple who'd had a big fight about groceries. She'd come in the house with the groceries on a Saturday morning and her husband started asking her questions about when the gardener was last at the house. The wife was super pissed because he hadn't offered to help with the groceries *and* she'd told him earlier in the week that the gardener wasn't coming that week.

All day long she seethed about what a thoughtless jerk her husband was and how he *never* listened to her and *always* forgot to ask to help with the groceries or other household chores. She ended up blowing up at him in a huge way and he, of course, got defensive: "I just asked a simple question about the gardener and you're blowing this WAY out of proportion!" He saw this as a "her" problem, while she was seeing this all as a "him" problem. The resentments continued to build on both sides and nothing was resolved.

Whenever you start using words like always and never, you're in a resentment. This reminds you of all the times you've felt ignored by your partner or like they're not thinking of you first. This isn't about this one time, it's about *all* the times you feel like they've screwed up with you before.

There are four main reasons why you don't forgive:

You don't forgive because you think it's

1. Forgetting. Maybe you think it means you just have to forgive and forget and you don't feel ready or *want* to move past the hurt.

2. Reconciliation. Maybe you're worried that your partner will think this means you're ready to have sex, laugh and be happy together again. You're thinking, "I'm not ready to be in a warm and intimate relationship with them and if I forgive them, they're going to think we're 'back to normal.'"

3. Condoning. Maybe you're thinking, "I can't have my partner believe that I think what they did is OK. If I forgive them, they'll just do it again. They should pay for what they did, and if I forgive them, there's no justice." Forgiveness and justice are *not* the same and seeking revenge or justice is a big problem and block to moving forward.

4. Weakness. Maybe you think it's a sign of weakness to forgive and that, if you forgive your partner,

they'll take total advantage of you and they'll do whatever they did over and over again because they think you won't stand up for yourself.

But forgiveness is none of these things. Forgiveness is leaving behind your revenge, hate and depression and rising to the next level of your life. Forgiveness is an incredible gift you give to yourself (that sounded corny, but it really is true). Your worst memories and thoughts don't just go away and get better. But YOU can get better.

> The big key to forgiveness is to know that... It's not about letting your partner off the hook. It's about letting yourself off the hook.

This is about you and not your partner. When you hold on to resentment, helplessness and anger, you're the one who suffers the most. Yes, you can make your partner miserable if you try—but is that really what you're going for? Has that ever made you happier in your relationship?

Letting hate, contempt or resentment breed is a very dangerous thing for both your mental and physical health, let alone the relationship with your partner.

Dr. Fred Luskin at Stanford University's Forgiveness Project[59] has been studying forgiveness for years. He's top dog when it comes to all things forgiveness.

His studies have found that people who learn forgiveness

- Suffer less depression
- Have less physical pain and symptoms

---

[59] https://learningtoforgive.com

- Experience less anger, stress and depression
- Improve appetite, sleep, energy and general well-being
- Become more hopeful, optimistic and compassionate

I'm sure you're able to see how having any of these things would positively impact and improve your relationship with yourself as well as your relationship with your partner.

But How Do I Forgive Exactly?

If you look at the research on forgiveness (and there's a lot), you'll find that the one thing that's often missing is understanding *how* to forgive. Lots of religions and well-meaning friends and family members talk about forgiveness, but they don't give you actual tools for making it happen.

As you've undoubtedly already noticed, just *saying,* "I forgive you," out loud doesn't really work. It's like the Forgiveness Fairy is supposed to come down, wave her magic wand, and you'll just suddenly feel differently. Your feelings aren't faucets, so you can't just turn them off and on at will. Forgiveness is like a muscle that needs attention and building to be effective. There are some specific things you can do to flex and build that muscle.

So, let's get to the steps to building your forgiveness muscle. There are five steps repeated in various forms in all the research,[60] so let's take a look at them now:

Step One: Make a Commitment

The first thing you need to do is make a commitment to yourself to do whatever you need to do to feel better. For-

---

60   https://www.amazon.com/Five-Steps-Forgiveness-Science-Forgiving/dp/0609609181

giveness is for you and not anyone else. Remind yourself that forgiveness might not mean reconciliation with the person that hurt you, and is never about condoning their actions. What you're after is finding peace, for yourself.

Step Two: There's No Closure

Don't wait for an apology. If you're waiting for someone else to apologize, it means that person has control over you. It means the ability to take action is out of your hands and in someone else's (someone who you're pissed at, no less). Isn't it time to put *you* back in the driver's seat? Isn't it time to take your power and the control back? How long are you going to let this person have a piece of yourself?

I know, I know, it can feel *so* good to be righteously angry. There's nothing better than being pissed when you're so sure you're right! But, you need to ask yourself, would you rather be correct or effective? Stop waiting for your partner to apologize and move on with your life. Closure is a bullshit term you have no time for. You don't get closure from someone else—you get it from yourself. Life's too short to wait.

Step Three: Acknowledge

Acknowledging the anger or hurt is step three. Acknowledge does NOT mean wallow in it. You've got to acknowledge it and not push it under the proverbial rug, but wallowing in it is bad, too.

Think about what happens when you talk about a negative thing over and over again. You start to feel like crap. You become negative yourself. Also, when you speak to 10 different people about something, you get 10 different opinions. It gets confusing to know your own mind. Instead, choose a special person to speak to (therapist, relative or friend you trust). Do this in a confined way and space. It shouldn't go on forever.

Step 4: Get Perspective

Now you're ready to get some perspective. If this is something that happened ten years ago, remember that you're not upset about something that's currently happening, but something old. The hurt is past, so if you're treating it like it's occurring now, that's a problem. Ask yourself some constructive questions, "When in your life have you coped with this the best?" "Who is the most supportive person you have?" "Did you learn anything good about yourself from this ordeal?"

Step 5: Stop the Replay

The fifth step is to stop replaying (and re-stimulating) the event! If you find yourself during your day remembering anything about this issue, I want you to practice breathing or meditation when the thoughts come up, so you can calm your nervous system and disengage your "fight or flight" reactions.

Remember, the more you replay a negative event or conversation in your head the more negative you're going to feel. That feeling gets entrenched in your neurocircuitry. Also, you start to twist what happened or what was said to make it closer to how you're feeling and you lose step #4 (perspective).

You need to ask yourself one question when you're tripping on something: "Is this helpful?" Is thinking about this over and over and replaying it like a movie in your head helping you? Are you feeling happier and lighter? I seriously doubt it. It doesn't help to do the replay—you're just focusing on being right, not happy. It's time to focus on being effective, not correct.

The 10 Keys to Being Happily Married

REAL-LIFE EXAMPLE

Lucy came to me because her husband, Jay, had cheated on her and she stated that she "just couldn't get over it." They'd been married for 11 years and had two sons ages 7 and 9. "How could he do this to me?" she said, "I hate him. I never want to see his face again."

I worked with Lucy for a few months and tried to introduce the steps of forgiveness to her at a few intervals, but she said that she just wasn't ready to forgive her husband. In the meantime, she was filled with rage and was lashing out "to make him hurt as much as he hurt me." She was telling her relatively young sons that their dad was a cheater and her anger was spilling out everywhere.

In about our fifth month of working together, she started to have headaches almost daily. After multiple doctors' visits it was determined that the headaches were due to her stress and clenching her jaw constantly. Around that time, one of her sons started having behavioral issues at school and started talking back to Lucy. It came out over time that he was being negatively impacted by all the anger, fighting and hostility at home. Lucy's angry outbursts had also affected their older son, who was becoming more withdrawn and spending more time in his room. Lucy also reported that two of her friends had told her that they didn't want to hear about Jay anymore and had been spending less and less time with her.

"My life is falling apart because of what he did! It's so unfair!" Lucy lamented to me. I worked with her over and over to try to show her that she was the one ruining her life, not Jay. She needed to take responsibility for how she was reacting to all this. Lucy became upset with me and stopped seeing me.

Almost a year later, I got a call from Lucy asking to come back. We met and she updated me on her life. "I'm miserable all the time. My children don't want to spend much time with me because I'm impatient and can't control my angry outbursts. Jay left me. Not even for another woman. He just left. Said he'd rather be alone than put up with my meanness anymore. We've started divorce proceedings. I can't sleep, I feel like my friends have all deserted me and I still believe it's all his fault.

"But, I've been thinking a lot about what you said—how I'm the one making myself miserable at this point. How I need to take responsibility for myself. I think I'm finally ready to do that, but I don't know if I can forgive him. I think some things just aren't forgivable."

I said to Lucy, "I want to tell you the story of Trisha Meili."

It's a story that hits close to my heart because I remember when it was being covered by every news outlet in the country. At the time of the story, Trisha was a 28-year-old investment banker at Salomon Brothers in New York City. She had graduated Phi Beta Kappa from Wellesley College and had two masters' degrees from Yale University. She regularly jogged six miles in Central Park after work to cope with the stress of her high-powered job. On April 19, 1989, she became known not as Trisha Meili, but as the "Central Park Jogger."

She was the victim of something called "wilding," which was a term used when a gang of young people went on a long and violent rampage in a public place, attacking people at random. Trisha was one of many who were attacked that night in and around Central Park. The story has changed over time, but it seems a gang of young men grabbed her, tied her up, repeatedly raped and sodomized her and beat her into a coma which lasted for almost two weeks. She had deep scalp lacerations and skull fractures. Her brain was swollen. Her eye had exploded from its socket. She had lost 80 percent of her blood and she was found unconscious and tied up, her body jerking uncontrollably because of massive brain damage.

Doctors questioned whether she would survive, and if she did, whether she would be in a vegetative state.

Twelve days after the attack, Meili surfaced from her coma. About four weeks later, she was told what happened; she remembered nothing about the attack. Incredibly, after five months of rehabilitation, she returned to her apartment and her job at Salomon Brothers. And she returned to running on weekends in Central Park.

In 1995, Meili ran the New York City Marathon, and the last leg goes through Central Park. It was a glorious day, she said, filling her with pride in her recovery and her physical, mental and emotional state.[61]

Somehow, she didn't give up and she didn't stay a victim.

Through her own sheer determination and willpower, she fought her way back and was, ultimately, able to return to work! Incredible! While she still liked her job, she was having trouble reconciling what happened to her. Was she just supposed to go back to her previous life as if nothing had happened?

She was angry. She had to figure out a way to make sense of the horrible thing that happened to her. She ended up forgiving whoever attacked her, but the real issue underneath it all was she had to forgive herself. She had been warned on multiple occasions not to jog alone but had decided, arrogantly she realized, that she'd be fine. It wasn't just a horrible time for her after she was attacked, but her family also "went through hell." All because she'd made this decision and thought nothing would ever happen to her.

---

61   http://www.centralparkjogger.com

She left Salomon in 1998 and became president of a New York nonprofit that offered no-interest loans to the working poor. She also gives her time as founding chair to Achilles International, whose mission is to enable people with disabilities to participate in mainstream athletics. She's also a sought-after motivational speaker. So, Trisha Meili *did* change after what happened to her.

I said to Lucy, "You can change, too. We all change with our life experiences. The difference between being victimized in some way and being a victim is epically huge. It's inevitable that things you don't want to happen, will happen. It's sometimes hard to remember that it's up to you to decide what to do with the experience. No one experience needs to define you. Choose what you're going to do with any situation. You can take something like infidelity in your relationship and turn it into a new beginning for the two of you.

"You can choose to make sense of it. Why did this happen? What does it mean? How can you use it to create something new in your life that helps move you forward?

"Forgiveness is a time of asking yourself questions, not of staying stuck in blame, doubt or rage. How can you move yourself and your life forward? What steps do you need to take to permanently move from whatever pain you're in, to living the life you want? If Trish Meili can forgive, so can you."

After a few more sessions of crying and attempts at forgiveness, Lucy finally really got it. She started to work this five-step process and her life changed radically. About three months later, she said in session, "I feel like I was locked in a prison before and didn't even realize it. I feel so much happier and lighter. I'm not sure if I can reconcile with Jay, but we're getting along so much better, my boys are happier and we're all connecting more. I'm not sure what's next, but life is so much better now."

No one is going to save you; *you* need to save you. Are you harboring resentments about an old relationship? Are you harboring resentments in your current relationship? It's time to move on and free yourself. I know it's not easy, but I'm telling you from my 30 years of experience that you won't have a happy life if you're mired in resentment, hate, hurt and seeking vengeance. It's just not possible.

> The things two people do to each other they remember. If they stay together, it's not because they forget; it's because they forgive.

ACTION TIPS

Tip #1:

Practice the Five-Step Forgiveness process outlined in this chapter. Start with something particular you want to forgive. For each of the five steps, write down what you're going to do in each step to ensure that you're on your way to forgiveness.

Tip #2:

This is *not* an exercise I recommend for anyone trying to forgive something violent such as rape, physical abuse or major verbal abuse. This is a forgiveness exercise that works well for interpersonal issues with your partner.

Take these steps:

- Think of your partner.
- Write down *one* thing you're grateful for about your partner, every day, for two weeks.
- It needs to be a different thing every day, so you might have to dig deep if you're really resentful or angry.
- Do it on your phone, write it on a notepad, whatever works for you. But write down one sentence with something you're grateful for about your partner. When you write it, *really feel it.*
- Allowing yourself to feel this gratitude will transform how you feel about the other person over time and it will transform how you feel about yourself (most importantly).

For you overachievers, if you like these Action Tips but want *more*, you can download my FREE Bonus Toolkit at *www.abbymedcalf.com/bonustoolkit*

CONCLUSION

In the end, there's one thing you have to decide in your relationship. Would you rather be correct or effective? You might be having an argument and you might be "right," but what is it getting you? You might also be right that fixing this relationship shouldn't just be up to you and that your partner should also be willing to do something. That's all well and good, but do you want a loving, supportive partner (effective) or do you want to be in a miserable relationship (correct)?

Shifting to this one question, asking if you want to be correct or effective, really changes the very nature of your engagement with your partner. It puts you on the same team instead of opposing sides of a power struggle.

The questions you want to consistently answer are, "What's my end game here? What am I trying to get done? What goal, both emotionally and physically, am I trying to accomplish?" Yes, maybe you're "correct" that your partner left his dirty socks in the middle of the floor (again), but do you want to fight about socks or have a fun night watching *Game of Thrones*? Instead of being correct, you could be effective and change your stance, your tone or the words that you use (or just hire a housekeeper). After all, if he keeps leaving his socks around even though you've "discussed" this (over and over), are you being effective and getting him to change his behavior or are you just feeling like a bitchy nag? You can be correct all day, but is this getting you to your goal of being understood and feeling appreciated?

The 10 Keys to Being Happily Married

> If you want to create a happy, connected, fulfilled relationship, it's time to let go of what your partner should be doing and focus only on what you are doing.

I know it's hard. If it were easy, you wouldn't need this book. But, isn't your relationship worth it?

I want you to take a minute and imagine a truly happy relationship. Picture yourself feeling relieved when you see your partner because you know everything is going to be OK. Picture yourself at ease and laughing with them. Picture the two of you having fun, enjoying rock star sex, confidently making decisions together, communicating effortlessly and feeling happy when your partner walks into the room. If I could guarantee that picture in your head, what would you be willing to do? Would you be willing to practice what you've learned here for the next three months? Doesn't that seem like a relatively small commitment and "price to pay" to live for the rest of your life in that happy relationship?

I have every faith that you can do this. Make it a priority and put your relationship first for a little while and watch it transform with your attention and intention.

Looking forward to hearing about all your success!

Abby

AUTHOR BIOGRAPHY

Abby is a psychologist and author who has been working with clients for over 30 years. She brings her unique background in business and counseling, humor, and being a **research junkie to her** work with individuals and couples. Abby is also a popular keynote speaker and presenter for such organizations as Google, Apple, AT&T, PG&E and American Airlines and has been interviewed on ABC and CBS news. You can check out her five-star podcast, *Relationships Made Easy* on iTunes, Stitcher or on her website, *abbymedcalf.com/podcast*.

Abby's mission is world peace. She believes that if every person in the world used her principles, they'd be happier, find meaning and feel more connected to themselves and others. People who felt like that would have no reason to fight, hate or bully. Following the logic, we'd end up with world peace.

When she's not writing books, speaking or seeing clients, Abby is an avid cook and loves feeding her partner, kids and friends. Although she now lives in the Bay Area of California, she can still be seen walking everywhere in stilettos and dreaming of eating pizza back in her hometown of New York City.